Rahu and Ketu

The Ultimate Guide to Two Opposite Lunar Nodes, Vedic Astrology, and Navagraha Worship

© Copyright 2024 - All rights reserved.

The content contained within this book may not be reproduced, duplicated, or transmitted without direct written permission from the author or the publisher.

Under no circumstances will any blame or legal responsibility be held against the publisher, or author, for any damages, reparation, or monetary loss due to the information contained within this book, either directly or indirectly.

Legal Notice:

This book is copyright protected. It is only for personal use. You cannot amend, distribute, sell, use, quote or paraphrase any part, or the content within this book, without the consent of the author or publisher.

Disclaimer Notice:

Please note the information contained within this document is for educational and entertainment purposes only. All effort has been executed to present accurate, up-to-date, reliable, and complete information. No warranties of any kind are declared or implied. Readers acknowledge that the author is not engaging in the rendering of legal, financial, medical, or professional advice. The content within this book has been derived from various sources. Please consult a licensed professional before attempting any techniques outlined in this book.

By reading this document, the reader agrees that under no circumstances is the author responsible for any losses, direct or indirect, that are incurred as a result of the use of the information contained within this document, including, but not limited to, errors, omissions, or inaccuracies.

Your Free Gift
(only available for a limited time)

Thanks for getting this book! If you want to learn more about various spirituality topics, then join Mari Silva's community and get a free guided meditation MP3 for awakening your third eye. This guided meditation mp3 is designed to open and strengthen ones third eye so you can experience a higher state of consciousness. Simply visit the link below the image to get started.

https://spiritualityspot.com/meditation

Or, Scan the QR code!

Table of Contents

INTRODUCTION 1
CHAPTER 1: INTRODUCTION TO VEDIC ASTROLOGY 3
CHAPTER 2: NAVAGRAHAS IN VEDIC ASTROLOGY 14
CHAPTER 3: RAHU: THE NORTH LUNAR NODE 31
CHAPTER 4: KETU: THE SOUTH LUNAR NODE 41
CHAPTER 5: THE LUNAR NODES AND THE NAKSHATRAS 51
CHAPTER 6: THE LUNAR NODES IN BIRTH CHARTS 62
CHAPTER 7: KARMIC PATTERNS 74
CHAPTER 8: REMEDIES FOR MALEFIC RAHU AND KETU 86
CHAPTER 9: NAVAGRAHA WORSHIP AND REMEDIES 95
CONCLUSION 105
GLOSSARY OF TERMS 107
HERE'S ANOTHER BOOK BY MARI SILVA THAT YOU MIGHT LIKE 109
YOUR FREE GIFT (ONLY AVAILABLE FOR A LIMITED TIME) 110
REFERENCES 111

Introduction

Do you want to understand the power of Rahu and Ketu in Vedic astrology? Are you looking for ways to mitigate their effect? Then this guide is the perfect resource.

Vedic astrology is no longer just a belief. It has gained immense popularity across the globe over the years due to its accurate predictions and effectiveness. As part of Vedic astrology, Rahu, and Ketu, the two shadow planets, hold immense importance due to their influence on people's lives. Although both are shadow planets, their impact is profound. This book dives deep into Rahu and Ketu, their nature, power, and how their influences.

The Moon's two nodes, Rahu and Ketu, are viewed as the most powerful planets in Vedic astrology. This comprehensive book provides everything to understand their influence on your life. This book covers the basics of Vedic astrology, Navagrahas (heavenly bodies), and Nakshatras (Lunar month).

Rahu and Ketu's position in your birth chart decides your karmic cycles. Likewise, the position of Rahu and Ketu in the natal chart's different houses determines the challenges and benefits your life path will bring. This book discusses the planetary position of Rahu and Ketu in the birth chart. Additionally, it covers the remedies for malefic Rahu and Ketu to help you mitigate their effects.

Rahu and Ketu's power varies according to their positions in your birth chart. If Rahu is placed positively, it brings prosperity, fame, respect, luxury, and fortune. But if it is adversely positioned, it can cause negative results like mental health issues, chronic diseases, and financial loss. This guide helps you identify Rahu and Ketu's favorable and unfavorable positions.

Lastly, this book covers the Navagraha worship and remedies for Rahu and Ketu you can use to appease them. These remedies are simple yet effective in reducing the negative impacts of Rahu and Ketu. Understanding Rahu and Ketu's positions in your birth chart provides an insightful understanding of your karmic cycles, life path, and critical challenges and opportunities you'll face in this lifetime.

Although Rahu and Ketu are shadow planets and have adverse effects, knowing how to balance their energies and leverage their positive energies, you can better understand your life journey and gain valuable insight into your past and future. By the end of this guide, you'll have a comprehensive understanding of the power of these two shadow planets.

Vedic astrology's ancient wisdom and Rahu and Ketu's power can positively transform you if you are willing to explore it. So, read on to understand Rahu and Ketu's influence in Vedic astrology.

Chapter 1: Introduction to Vedic Astrology

Vedic astrology is a science dating back thousands of years. It is a complex system of interpreting the stars' and planets' movements and positions. With its roots in ancient India, Vedic astrology has recently gained popularity worldwide as people seek a deeper understanding of themselves and their place in the universe. Unlike Western astrology, which focuses on the sun signs, Vedic astrology takes a more holistic approach, examining the entire birth chart and the interplay between planets and constellations.

Practitioners can gain insight into a person's personality, life path, and destiny via this system. There is a wealth of information to uncover and explore within this fascinating field; this chapter provides an overview of the history and origins, its influences from Hinduism, and its components. It discusses symbols and symbolism of the zodiac signs and houses according to Vedic astrology. By the end of this chapter, readers will better understand the fundamentals of Vedic astrology.

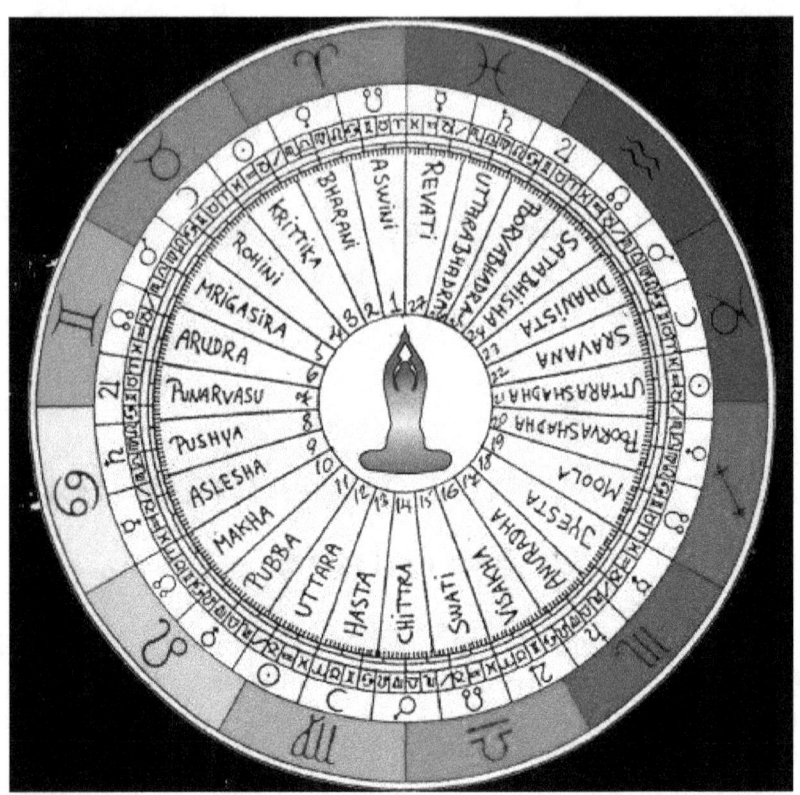

Vedic Astrology Chart.
See page for author, CC BY-SA 4.0 <https://creativecommons.org/licenses/by-sa/4.0>, via Wikimedia Commons:
https://commons.wikimedia.org/wiki/File:Astrologia_V%C3%A9dica_2018.jpg

Exploring the Fundamental Differences between Vedic and Western Astrology

Astrology is a fascinating and complex subject studied and applied in various cultures for centuries. While the principles of astrology remain the same across different systems, the approach and methodology of interpreting astrology vary from one culture to another. Vedic astrology and Western astrology are two systems that differ fundamentally. This section explores the primary differences between Vedic and Western astrology and highlights the strengths and weaknesses of both systems.

Origin and History

One significant difference between these two systems is their origin and history. Vedic astrology, known as *Jyotish*, is based on ancient

Hindu scriptures and has been practiced for over 5,000 years. It is deeply rooted in Indian culture and influenced by various Hindu philosophical concepts. In contrast, Western astrology originated in ancient Greece and Rome and is based on the planets' and stars' movements. The Western system has evolved, influenced by various cultural and religious factors.

Vedic and Western astrology have their strengths and weaknesses. While Western astrology is more precise in timing, Vedic astrology provides a deeper understanding of a person's life and destiny. The Vedic system is better at predicting karma and destiny, while the Western system is more suited for analyzing current situations. In addition, Vedic astrology is not limited to the twelve zodiac signs like Western astrology. Instead, it considers the placement of nine planets and twenty-seven constellations, called Nakshatras. The Vedic system also considers each chart's Bhavas or houses.

Zodiac System

Another significant difference between Vedic and Western astrology is their zodiac system. The Western system follows the tropical zodiac, which is based on the Sun's position at birth. It is defined by the four seasons, solstices, and equinoxes. On the other hand, the Vedic system uses the sidereal zodiac based on the actual position of the stars. The zodiac signs in Vedic astrology are about 23 degrees apart from the Western system, often resulting in a different interpretation of a person's birth chart. Vedic astrology is focused on the planet's position in relation to the stars. Western astrology is more concerned with the planets' relation to Earth.

Planetary Rulerships

The planetary rulerships in Vedic and Western astrology also differ. In Western astrology, each zodiac sign is ruled by a particular planet. In contrast, Vedic astrology assigns rulership to the two luminaries, the Sun and Moon, including the two shadowy planets, Rahu and Ketu. Moreover, while the Western system places significant emphasis on the Sun sign, the Vedic system considers the Moon's position equally important, if not more. The Nakshatras in Vedic astrology is ruled by particular planets, adding another layer to interpreting a person's birth chart. It is worth noting that the Vedic system does not assign a planet to each house, as Western astrology does.

Predictive Techniques

Both systems have different predictive techniques. For example, Vedic astrology uses a complex system of Dashas, or planetary periods, which divides an individual's life into segments and analyzes the different planet's influences during those periods. On the other hand, Western astrology uses various predictive techniques like transits, progressions, and solar returns, analyzing the planet's movements and their influence on a person's life.

Astrology is a vast subject encompassing various systems, symbols, and techniques. Vedic and Western astrology differ fundamentally; however, they provide valuable insight into an individual's strengths, weaknesses, and life path. Vedic astrology offers a more holistic approach, considering the influence of luminaries and shadowy planets, and uses a complex system of planetary periods for predictive analysis. Western astrology, on the other hand, focuses on the Sun sign and uses various predictive techniques like transits, progressions, and solar returns.

Unveiling the Fascinating History and Origins of Vedic Astrology

Astrology, the art of interpreting the relationship between celestial bodies and human affairs, has been part of human culture for millennia. One of the most ancient and profound systems of astrology is Vedic astrology. Its origin can be traced back to the Vedas, the oldest sacred Hinduism text. Vedic astrology has guided people for centuries and is still prevalent in India and other parts of the world. This section unveils Vedic astrology's fascinating history and origins and explores why it's still relevant today.

Origins of Vedic Astrology

Vedic astrology's birth can be traced back to the ancient sages of India. The Rishis believed the position and movement of celestial bodies could influence human lives. So, they studied the stars and planets for years and observed their effects on people's health, wealth, and relationships. The Vedas consist of four parts: Rigveda, Samaveda, Yajurveda, and Atharvaveda. The Atharvaveda references astrology, believed to be the oldest book on astrology. The Rishis formulated a system that could determine the favorable and unfavorable times for specific actions like marriage, travel, or starting a business. They called it "Jyotish," or the science of light.

Structure and Elements of Vedic Astrology

Vedic Astrology has unique rules, methods, and calculations. The system divides the ecliptic plane into 27 equal parts, each owned by a planet or star. These divisions, or Nakshatras, are further subdivided into smaller pieces, each represented by a deity. The position of planets in these Nakshatras and their movements form the horoscope chart. The chart consists of 12 houses, each representing an aspect of human life. The system uses seven planets, including the Sun, Moon, Mars, Mercury, Jupiter, Venus, Saturn, and the two shadow planets, Rahu and Ketu.

The Significance of Vedic Astrology Today

Vedic Astrology's relevance today can be seen in the ever-growing interest worldwide. People rely on astrology to gain insight into their futures, situational guidance, passion, sexuality, relationships, and career paths. Horoscopes are used to gain insight into a life where people feel loss or unrest. With a comprehensive horoscope reading, individuals can understand their needs, desires, and talents. You can learn more about your personality, strengthen your relationships, and improve your career path with Vedic Astrology's help.

How Vedic Astrology Works

Vedic astrology examines and analyzes a person's karmic and cosmic state and the present, past, and future. The more intricate and accurate the calculations based on the birth details, the more precise the reading of a person's personality and cosmic influences. Planets' placement in Nakshatras and the houses in which they reside have substantial implications on the individual's nature and life. Vedic astrology can determine auspicious times for rituals, new beginnings, and essential life decisions.

Vedic astrology's history and origins are fascinating and show how astrology has been ingrained in human culture. Its structure and elements are complex yet precise and have helped countless individuals gain insights into their lives and improve their futures. The relevance and popularity of Vedic astrology today showcase its continued significance in the modern world. Whether you are a believer or a skeptic, understanding the history and concepts of Vedic astrology is a fascinating and worthwhile journey.

The Intricate Influence of Hinduism on Vedic Astrology

India is an ancient civilization that contributed to developing the ancient practice of Vedic astrology, Jyotish. Vedic astrology has its roots in Hinduism and is an integral part of Indian culture. It provides insights into life and can help people understand their potential and limitations. Hinduism and Vedic astrology are deeply intertwined, so understanding Hinduism is crucial to understanding the essence of Vedic astrology. This section discusses the influence of Hinduism on Vedic astrology and its significance in people's lives.

Vedic astrology's fundamental principles were laid out in the ancient text, Brihat Parashara Hora Shastra. This text contains a wealth of knowledge on different aspects of Vedic astrology, including the importance of Hinduism. According to Vedic astrology, each person's life is a journey determined by the cosmic forces and energy of the universe. Therefore, the various planets, constellations, and their placements can influence a person's life, and Hinduism is crucial in defining the relationship between these forces and energy.

Hinduism's influence on Vedic astrology is evident in the numerous deities and demigods worshipped. Central to Vedic astrology, the nine planets are associated with different deities from Hindu mythology. For example, the Sun is associated with Lord Surya, the Moon with Lord Chandra, and Saturn with Lord Shani. These deities are believed to influence the planets, directly affecting a person's life.

Hinduism substantially determines the auspicious and inauspicious times for various activities. For instance, according to Vedic astrology, certain planets favor specific activities, like getting married, starting a new business, or buying a house. Furthermore, festivals like Diwali are celebrated based on Vedic astrology principles. For instance, the Diwali festival celebrates Lord Rama's return to Ayodhya after defeating the demon king, Ravana, and coincides with the planets' movements.

Another way Hinduism influences Vedic astrology is through Yagyas or Homas practices. Yagya is a Vedic ritual where offerings are made to a specific deity to invoke their blessings to help overcome obstacles in life and bring good fortune. Vedic astrology places great importance on Yagyas and considers them excellent for improving a person's life. They are performed based on the planetary positions in the natal chart, and the deity is chosen to coincide with the planet causing the problem.

The intricate relationship between these two ancient practices is fascinating, and the more you delve into them, the more you observe their interconnectedness. Vedic astrology is a powerful tool offering valuable insights into life, and understanding Hinduism's role provides greater depth and meaning to these insights. Astrology has evolved over millennia, but the link between Hinduism and Vedic astrology remains strong and continues to influence people worldwide.

Components of the Vedic Astrological Chart

The Vedic astrological chart, based on ancient Indian astrology, Jyotish Shastra, is an overall system studied, analyzed, and written about by experts for many years. The Vedic astrological chart comprises several vital components creating an in-depth profile of an individual's personality, traits, strengths, and weaknesses. This section dives deeper into the three main elements of the Vedic astrological chart, including zodiac signs, Navagrahas or planets, and Bhavas or houses.

Zodiac Signs or Rashis

The Vedic astrological chart uses 12 zodiac signs or Rashis to create a complete picture of an individual's personality traits. These signs are Aries, Taurus, Gemini, Cancer, Leo, Virgo, Libra, Scorpio, Sagittarius, Capricorn, Aquarius, and Pisces. An individual's zodiac sign is determined by the position of the Sun and the Moon at birth. Each sign has unique positive and negative traits, attributes, and tendencies. For example, Aries is known for being headstrong and impulsive, while Taurus is known for being stubborn and hardworking. Understanding people's zodiac signs can provide valuable insight into their personalities and help them make better life decisions.

These zodiac signs are connected to the Hindu deities, and each sign has a particular god associated with it. For instance, Aries is associated with Lord Hanuman, Taurus with Lord Varaha, and Gemini with Lord Shiva. Knowing the Hindu deities associated with each sign gives additional insight into your personality and life purpose. In addition, the symbolism and mythology associated with each sign help individuals become more aware of their inner potential and better understand their challenges.

Navagrahas or Planets

The Vedic astrological chart includes nine planets or Navagrahas: the Sun, Moon, Mars, Mercury, Jupiter, Venus, Saturn, Rahu, and Ketu.

Each planet has unique meanings and attributes and impacts an individual's life. For instance, Mars represents aggression and action, Venus represents love and relationships, and Saturn represents discipline and hard work. An individual's Navagraha position at birth determines their personality traits. Therefore, understanding Navagrahas helps individuals make decisions based on their strengths, weaknesses, and personal characteristics.

If the Navagrahas are not properly aligned, they can cause problems in an individual's life. Special remedial measures are taken to improve this alignment, like chanting mantras or wearing certain gemstones. The Navagrahas associate with the nine planets and Hindu deities like the zodiac signs are, and understanding this connection provides further insight into your life. The Navagrahas are essential in Vedic astrology, but their influence is much more complex and must be studied in greater detail.

Bhavas or Houses

The Vedic astrological chart includes 12 Bhavas or houses, which are interconnected and depict specific areas of an individual's life. The first Bhava represents the self, while the 12th Bhava represents liberation or Moksha. The second Bhava represents finances, while the seventh represents marriage and partnerships. Each Bhava is crucial in an individual's life and determines the energies surrounding them. Understanding the Bhavas can help individuals better decide, plan their life, and achieve their aspirations.

The chart is a powerful system offering valuable insight into an individual's personality and life path. Understanding the Vedic astrological chart's components - including the zodiac signs or Rashis, Navagrahas or planets, and Bhavas (houses) - helps individuals understand themselves more deeply and make better life decisions. Individuals can unlock their potential using this ancient system and achieve prosperity, joy, and fulfillment.

The Symbolism of Zodiac Signs and Houses According to Vedic Astrology

Astrology has been a fascinating topic since ancient times and is an integral part of life today. One of the most exciting aspects of astrology is the symbolism of each zodiac sign and house. Vedic astrology offers insight into cosmic energies and how they impact individuals' lives. This section explores the symbolism of each zodiac sign and house according to Vedic astrology.

Aries (Mesh) - First House: Aries is represented by a ram, symbolizing strength, courage, and leadership. Mars, the planet of action and energy, rules it. The first house is called the House of Self and represents an individual's personality, physical appearance, and characteristics. This house is associated with new beginnings, self-expression, and independence. If well-aspected, it can bring luck and success. The first house, known as the *Ascendant* or *Lagna*, is the most important in a natal chart, as it sets the stage for the rest of the graph.

Taurus (Vrishabha) - Second House: Taurus is symbolized by a bull, representing steadiness, stubbornness, and endurance. Venus, the planet of beauty, love, and luxury, rules it. The second house is associated with wealth, possessions, and material resources. This house represents an individual's values, self-worth, and ability to accumulate wealth and resources. A well-aspected second house can bring stability, abundance, and comfort.

Gemini (Mithuna) - Third House: Gemini is represented by twins, symbolizing versatility, communication, and curiosity. Mercury, the planet of communication and intellect, rules it. The third house is associated with communication, learning, and mental abilities. It represents an individual's ability to express themselves, curiosity and thirst for knowledge, and relationships with siblings and close friends. A well-aspected third house can bring intelligence, intuition, and clarity.

Cancer (Karkata) - Fourth House: Cancer is symbolized by a crab, representing emotions, sensitivity, and protectiveness. The Moon, the planet of emotions and intuition, rules it. The fourth house, the House of Home and Family, represents an individual's emotional foundation, roots, and traditions. This house is associated with an individual's family, childhood, and security. A well-aspected fourth house can bring emotional security, strong family connections, and a sense of belonging.

Leo (Simha) - Fifth House: Leo is represented by a lion, symbolizing confidence, creativity, and self-expression. The Sun, the planet of vitality and self-expression, rules it. The fifth house is associated with creativity, self-expression, and pleasure. It represents an individual's passion and creativity, ability to take risks and showcase their talents, and relationships with children and romantic partners. A well-aspected fifth house can bring abundance, joy, and success.

Virgo (Kanya) - Sixth House: Virgo is symbolized by a maiden, representing practicality, precision, and health. Mercury, the planet of intellect and communication, rules it. The sixth house is associated with health, work, and service. This house represents an individual's ability to be productive and organized daily, commit to service and duty, and stay healthy. A well-aspected sixth house can bring efficiency, productivity, and health.

Libra (Tula) - Seventh House: Libra is represented by a scale, symbolizing balance, harmony, and relationships. Venus, the planet of beauty and love, rules it. The seventh house is associated with relationships, partnerships, and marriage. This house represents an individual's ability to get along with others, relationships with their significant others, and the qualities they seek in a partner. A well-aspected seventh house can bring strong relationships, harmony, and balance.

Scorpio (Vrishchika) - Eighth House: Scorpio is symbolized by a scorpion, representing transformation, death, and rebirth. Mars, the planet of action and energy, rules it. The eighth house is associated with death, rebirth, transformation, and the occult. This house represents an individual's ability to confront complex issues, a profound understanding of life's mysteries, and interest in the mysterious aspects of existence. A well-aspected eighth house can bring profound insight and personal transformation.

Sagittarius (Dhanus) - Ninth House: Sagittarius is represented by an archer, symbolizing ambition, spirituality, and higher learning. Jupiter, the planet of expansion and wisdom, rules it. The ninth house is associated with higher education, travel, philosophy, and religion. This house represents an individual's ability to broaden their horizons through education, travel, and spiritual beliefs and values. A well-aspected ninth house can bring wisdom, knowledge, and spiritual understanding.

Capricorn (Makara) - Tenth House: Capricorn is symbolized by a sea-goat, representing ambition, responsibility, and career. Saturn, the planet of structure and limitations, rules it. The tenth house is associated with employment, public status, and reputation. This house represents an individual's ability to succeed in their field or profession and their qualities to show leadership. A well-aspected tenth house can bring career success, respect, and recognition.

Aquarius (Kumbha) - Eleventh House: Aquarius is represented by a man pouring water, symbolizing humanitarianism, friendship, and group consciousness. Saturn, the planet of structure and limitations, rules it. The eleventh house is associated with friendships, hopes, and wishes. This house represents an individual's ability to build solid connections and social networks, their capacity for idealism and altruism, and hopes for their future. A well-aspected eleventh house can bring social success and strong friendships.

Pisces (Meena) - Twelfth House: Pisces is symbolized by two fish, representing imagination, intuition, and compassion. Jupiter, the planet of expansion and wisdom, rules it. The twelfth house is associated with hidden enemies, secrets, and self-undoing. This house represents an individual's capacity for compassion and understanding, potential for creative imagination, and vulnerability to ill fortune. It reflects the spiritual growth and knowledge they seek. A well-aspected twelfth house can bring spiritual enlightenment and a strong intuitive connection to the divine.

Vedic astrology provides a deeper understanding of the symbolism of each zodiac sign and house, offering insight into personality, values, and relationships. By exploring these cosmic energies, you can better understand yourself and others and how to use these energies to lead a fulfilling life. Whether you believe in astrology or not, it can be a tool for self-discovery and understanding the world around you. So, the next time you look up at the stars, consider their powerful impact on people's lives and look closer at each zodiac sign and house's symbolism.

This chapter introduced the basics of Vedic astrology and how Hinduism has dramatically influenced it. It discussed the components of a Vedic Astrological Chart, including the zodiac signs or Rashis, the Navagrahas or planets, and the Bhavas or houses. Lastly, the chapter elaborated on each concept and provided an overview of each zodiac sign and house's symbolism, according to Vedic astrology. With this knowledge, you can explore your Vedic astrological chart's profound meaning and better understand life and how it is affected by the planets. Now that you're armed with this information, your decisions can lead to a more fulfilling life.

Chapter 2: Navagrahas in Vedic Astrology

In Vedic astrology, the Navagrahas are the nine celestial bodies pivotal in life. Each graha (one of the nine planets in the Navagrahas) represents a specific energy with the power to influence emotions, behavior, and destiny. From the Sun's fiery energy to Saturn's reflective nature, each graha holds a unique place in the cosmic picture. Understanding the Navagrahas and their impact on life can help you navigate the twists and turns life throws your way quickly and gracefully.

All passionate believers in Vedic astrology's power would agree that the Navagrahas are integral to their lives. This chapter delves into each of the seven planets to get to know them better. It explores their mythological background, symbolism, and characteristics. Furthermore, it analyzes the planetary cycles and periods each planet undergoes and their impact on an individual's life path and experiences. Lastly, it discusses the effects of planetary combinations and aspects of the Navagraha.

Sun (Surya)

Surya, the Sun Navagraha.

The essential component of Vedic astrology is Navagraha, the nine planets with astronomical and astrological influence over human life. This section explores the planetary impact of the Sun or Surya, one of the Vedic tradition's most prominent and revered Navagraha. It delves into the mythological background, characteristics, symbolism, planetary cycles and periods, and the impact on an individual's life path. So, fasten your seat belts as you embark on an enlightening journey into Indian astrology.

Mythological Background

In ancient Hindu mythology, the Sun or Surya is considered the deity of truth, courage, and power. Surya is the son of sage Kashyapa and Aditi, the mother of the gods. He is considered the father of Yama, the god of death, and the teacher of the King of gods, Indra. He is often depicted riding his chariot through the sky, pulled by seven horses representing the seven colors of the rainbow. Surya's importance in Hinduism is seen in numerous prayers and hymns dedicated to him, like the Aditya Hridayam, recited for health, prosperity, and success.

Surya's Significance in Vedic Culture and Astrology

Surya's significance in Vedic astrology manifests in numerous ways. Surya is the source of life and the center of the solar system. Hence, it is associated with vitality, energy, and willpower. It represents the soul (or Jeevatma) and bestows intelligence, creativity, and leadership qualities. Surya means the father figure in the horoscope and rules over the Leo zodiac sign, ruling the fifth house. In an individual's chart, the placement and strength of Surya determine the degree of success, fame, and recognition likely to be achieved in life.

Characteristics and Symbolism

Each planet is associated with characteristics and symbolism in Vedic astrology. Surya is a hot and temperamental planet, representing the fire element. It is known as the *Karaka planet* or the planet representing a particular aspect of life. Surya means ego, self-esteem, and self-confidence. Surya rules the body's right eye, heart, and digestive system. Classically, Surya is depicted with four arms and holding a lotus, a disc, a conch shell, and a mace. The lotus represents purity. The disc indicates the light of knowledge, the conch shell symbolizes victory, and the mace represents strength.

Planetary Cycles and Periods

Each planet has a specific transit period in Vedic astrology, determining the various auspicious or inauspicious phases of an individual's life. Surya's transit across multiple zodiac signs and houses can significantly change lives. Surya is believed to be exalted in Aries's zodiac sign and debilitated in Libra's zodiac sign. The prolonged Surya Mahadasha (significant period) can bring in name, fame, and wealth.

Impact on a Life's Path

Surya's placement in an individual's horoscope in Vedic astrology can determine their life path and personality traits. Surya's strength in the horoscope can evaluate the individual's confidence, courage, and leadership qualities. It can indicate their success in politics, government, finance, and creative pursuits. The weak placement of Surya can lead to various health-related issues and an overall lack of vitality and energy in life.

The Sun or Surya is a significant Navagraha in Vedic astrology, influencing various aspects of an individual's life. It represents the source of life and energy, vitality, and willpower. The placement and strength of Surya in an individual's horoscope can determine their success, fame, and recognition in life. Understanding the role and impact of Navagraha in your horoscope helps you make informed decisions and enable a more fulfilling and joyful life.

The Moon (Chandra)

Chandra, the Moon Navagraha.
https://commons.wikimedia.org/wiki/File:Chandra_the_Moon,_by_Ravi_Varma_Press.jpg

Vedic astrology has been practiced for centuries to understand and interpret the influence of celestial bodies on human lives. Among the nine heavenly bodies or Navagraha in Vedic astrology, the Moon or Chandra is significant because of its association with emotions, moods, and consciousness. This section explores the mythology, significance, characteristics, symbolism, and planetary cycles of the Moon in Vedic astrology.

Mythological Background

In Hindu mythology, the Moon or Chandra is the son of sage Atri and Anusuya, known as Soma, the god of the nectar of immortality. According to legend, Chandra was married to the 27 daughters of Daksha, the god of creation. However, he showed more love and affection to Rohini, who was the most beautiful. Daksha cursed Chandra to suffer from a wasting disease. Later, Lord Shiva gave him the elixir of life, curing him of the disease but also causing him to wax and wane.

The Moon's Significance in Vedic Culture and Astrology

The Moon is associated with feminine energy, fertility, and creativity in Vedic culture and is considered the ruler of the mind, emotions, and mental states. The position and movement of the Moon in relation to the other Navagraha impact an individual's personality, behavior, and destiny. It governs the physical body fluid and menstrual cycles.

Characteristics and Symbolism

The Moon is associated with the water element, and its ruling deity is the goddess, Parvati. It represents the essence of living beings, and its waxing and waning symbolize the cyclical nature of life, death, and rebirth. The Moon is characterized by its soft, sensitive, emotional, and nurturing spirit and is associated with intelligence, memory, and intuition.

Planetary Cycles and Periods

The Moon moves through all the 12 zodiac signs in 27.3 days, called a lunar month or Nakshatra. Each Nakshatra has a unique energy, and the Moon's position in these Nakshatras at birth influences an individual's traits and characteristics. The Moon affects the women's monthly menstrual cycles, and its position in the birth chart determines a person's emotional, mental, and psychological patterns.

Impact on a Life's Path

The Moon's placement in a birth chart influences an individual's emotional nature, mental tendencies, and creative expression. People with a strong Moon influence are often intuitive, imaginative, artistic, and empathic. They are sensitive to others' emotions and have fluctuating moods and impressions. The Moon influences a person's relationship with their mother, family, and home and is significant in their careers in emotions, psychology, healthcare, and art.

The Moon, or Chandra, is an essential celestial body in Vedic astrology, and its influence on human life cannot be understated. It represents feminine energy and the essence of life. Understanding the Moon's position, cycles, and impact on a birth chart can help people navigate their emotions, psychological patterns, and life path. By honoring and aligning with the Moon's energies, people can tap into their intuition, creativity, and nurturing nature and find balance and harmony.

Mars (Mangal)

Mangal, the Mars Navagraha.
British Museum, CC BY-SA 4.0 <https://creativecommons.org/licenses/by-sa/4.0>, via Wikimedia Commons:
https://commons.wikimedia.org/wiki/File:One_of_the_Indian_planets,_probably_Mangala_(the_Mars)_-_relief_from_the_British_Museum.jpg

The Navagraha system holds immense significance in Hindu mythology and astrology. One of these heavenly bodies is Mars, known as *Mangal*.

Besides being the god of War in Hindu mythology, this planet bears significant meaning and influence in astrology. This section discusses the mythological background, significance in Vedic culture, characteristics and symbolism, planetary cycles and periods, and impacts on Mars's life path in Navagraha in Vedic astrology.

Mythological Background

According to Hindu mythology, Mars is the son of the goddess Earth and sage Kashyap. He is the god of War, and it is believed he was born with a weapon in his hand. He is known to be fierce, assertive, and aggressive, considered a lover of arts and beauty, and associated with feminine energy. Mars is the god who can make an individual courageous, passionate, and ambitious to achieve goals.

Mars's Significance in Vedic Culture and Astrology

Mars or Mangal holds an important place in Vedic astrology and culture. It is considered a beneficial planet that can propel individuals to succeed. The planet is known to bestow energy, vitality, and inspiration on those who seek it. It is the protector of dharma or righteousness. In Hindu culture, Tuesday is dedicated to Mars, and people perform pujas and rituals to seek blessings from the planet.

Characteristics and Symbolism

Mars is a fiery planet signifying courage, aggression, passion, and drive. The planet represents vitality, strength, and energy and is associated with the fire element and rules over Aries and Scorpio. The planet is represented by red and symbolized by a circle with an arrow pointing upward and to the right. The symbol represents the upward direction and dynamic force of the planet.

Planetary Cycles and Periods

Mars takes around 45- 47 days to transit through one sign and approximately 1.5 years to cover all 12 zodiac signs. It has a retrograde period when it appears to be moving backward, which lasts about 80 days. Mars can cause more harm than good during retrograde, leading to conflicts, accidents, and injuries.

Impact on a Life's Path

Mars significantly impacts an individual's life path as it governs energy, strength, and passion. It can make an individual courageous, assertive, and ambitious. Negatively, Mars can make an individual aggressive, impulsive, and restless. In medical astrology, Mars is associated with the head, blood, and muscular system. Therefore, an affliction to Mars in the birth chart can lead to health issues in these areas.

Mars or Mangal is a significant planet in Navagraha in Vedic Astrology. This planet is known to bestow energy, vitality, and inspiration on those who seek it. The planet is a symbol of courage, passion, and strength. It governs Aries and Scorpio, and Tuesday is dedicated to it. Knowing the characteristics and impacts of Mars can help individuals harness the positive energies of this planet. Seeking blessings and performing pujas for Mars helps individuals lead healthy and prosperous lives.

Mercury (Budha)

Budha, the Mercury Navagraha.
https://commons.wikimedia.org/wiki/File:Budha_graha.JPG

Vedic astrology is known worldwide for its accurate predictions and methods that have stood the test of time. This section delves into the third graha in Navagraha: Mercury (Budha). It explores its mythology, significance in Vedic culture and astrology, characteristics, symbolism, planetary cycles and periods, and impact on an individual's life path.

Mythological Background

Mercury is believed to be the son of the Moon and Rohini, one of his 28 wives, in Hindu mythology. According to legend, Budha was born a prince who renounced his position to become an outstanding intellectual and scholar. He's known in the scriptures as the god of intelligence. His association with education and learning is considered one of the central themes of Mercury.

Mercury's Significance in Vedic Culture and Astrology

Budha is considered one of the most critical planets in Vedic astrology. It impacts people's intellectual capacity, communication skills, wit, and humor. Those born under this planet's influence are usually articulate, intelligent, and quick-witted. They have a knack for learning and adapting to new situations.

Characteristics and Symbolism

Mercury is represented as a young man with a muscular build, sporting a mustache, and adorned with precious gems. He holds a sword and a shield and is seated on a lion. The planet is related to logic, reasoning, communication, and commerce. It is essential in business and trading and is believed to represent mathematics, science, and research.

Planetary Cycles and Periods

The planetary cycle of Mercury lasts for 88 days in Vedic astrology. The planet is close to the Sun, and its transit period usually varies from two weeks to a month. It's believed that during its retrograde, which occurs three to four times a year, it's best to avoid making important decisions or signing contracts, as the planet's energy is at its lowest ebb.

Impact on a Life's Path

A strong Mercury in an individual's horoscope means they will likely have a successful career in fields requiring excellent communication and analytical skills. Those with a weak Mercury could experience setbacks in their professional lives, fail to communicate effectively, or struggle with mental confusion. People born under Buddha's influence are blessed with quick reflexes, sharp minds, and tremendous problem-solving abilities. Furthermore, it is the planet of positivism, bringing good luck and prosperity to those born under its influence.

Mercury, or Buddha, is an essential planet in Vedic astrology, holding a pivotal role in a person's intellectual growth, communication skills, and professional life. The planet's impact is crucial concerning an individual's analytical thinking and problem-solving skills, making it an essential component of their personality. Understanding the planet and its cycles helps you better understand its significance in life and navigate its impact to unlock tremendous growth and achievement.

Jupiter (Guru or Brihaspati)

Guru (Brihaspati), the Jupiter Navagraha.
https://commons.wikimedia.org/wiki/File:Brihaspati_graha_(crop).jpg

Jupiter, or Guru, is one of the most prominent planets in Vedic astrology. The planet is regarded as the most beneficial planet in the solar system, symbolizing wisdom, fortune, and knowledge. This section explores Jupiter's significance in Vedic culture, astrology, characteristics, and symbolism. It delves into the planetary cycles and periods and explores their impact on the life path of an individual.

Mythological Background

Jupiter is associated with the Guru, meaning teacher, and Brihaspati, who is regarded as the priest of the gods in Hindu mythology. According to Hindu mythology, the planet was born of the sage Angiras. Jupiter is associated with the god Chandra. The planet dispels darkness and ignorance and blesses individuals with wisdom.

Jupiter's Significance in Vedic Culture and Astrology

In Vedic culture, Guru or Jupiter is regarded as the most influential and significant planet of Navagrahas. It represents knowledge, intelligence, and spirituality. The planet governs the liver, the pituitary gland, and the fat metabolism in the body. Jupiter's placement in an individual's horoscope signifies the individual's spiritual path and pursuit of knowledge in Vedic astrology.

Characteristics and Symbolism

Jupiter is represented as the giant planet in the solar system and appears as a bright star in the sky. The planet is associated with the color yellow and the yellow sapphire gemstone. The Jupiter symbol is a crescent placed above a cross, symbolizing stability and expansion. Jupiter's nature is considered benevolent, signifying growth, knowledge, and evolution.

Planetary Cycles and Periods

Jupiter takes around 13 months to complete its orbit around the Sun. The planet's cycles and periods impact an individual's life path profoundly. Its position in an individual's horoscope determines their inclination toward spirituality, fortune, knowledge, and overall growth. Jupiter returns to its original position every 12 years, and this period is referred to as the "Jupiter Return."

Impact on a Life's Path

Jupiter is known as the planet of fortune, and its position in an individual's horoscope influences their fortune. Individuals with a strong Jupiter influence are more optimistic, intuitive, and inclined toward spiritual pursuits. Jupiter signifies wealth, success, and abundance. Conversely, a weak Jupiter indicates a lack of direction, confusion, and focus on an individual's life path.

Jupiter, or Guru, is one of the most significant planets of Navagrahas in Vedic astrology. Its influence on an individual reflects their fortune, expansion, and growth. Through its powerful cycles and periods, Jupiter shapes an individual's life path, steering them toward spiritual pursuits, success, and abundance. Understanding the power of Jupiter creates a life of positive growth, quantity, and fulfillment.

Venus (Shukra)

Shukra, the Venus Navagraha.
https://commons.wikimedia.org/wiki/File:Shukra_graha.JPG

Astrology, as a science, has been prominent in Indian culture for many years. Venus is crucial in shaping individuals' destinies in Vedic astrology. This section explores Venus (Shukra) and its significance in

Vedic culture and astrology.

Mythological Background

In Hindu mythology, Venus is associated with the goddess of beauty and love, Shukra. According to legends, Shukra was one of the Ashtadikpalakas (the eight guardians of the cardinal directions) and was the Guru to the Asuras (demons). It is believed that Shukra was responsible for bringing the asuras back to life after. Later, Shukra became one of the Navagrahas, and Venus became its astrological representation.

Venus's Significance in Vedic Culture and Astrology

Vedic culture considers Venus the planet of love, beauty, and luxury. It rules over materialistic pleasures, art, music, dance, and creativity. People born under Venus's influence are attracted to aesthetics and possess pleasant personalities. Venus is the significator or ruler of the second and seventh houses in astrology. It is considered a benefic planet, and its placement and aspects in a birth chart indicate favorable outcomes in love, relationships, finance, and creativity.

Characteristics and Symbolism

A beautiful woman represents Venus or Shukra, mounted on an antelope or parrot chariot. The planet epitomizes femininity, beauty, love, and charity. It reflects an individual's instincts toward love, relationships, material possessions, and creative pursuits. Venus is said to have a magnetic effect and governs aesthetics and attraction. It bestows sensuality, charm, grace, and refinement, making an individual's personality charming; people are usually attracted to them.

Planetary Cycles and Periods

Venus completes a zodiac cycle in approximately 225 days and stays in one sign for about a month. The period of Venus is called the Shukra Dasha in astrology. During this period, Venus blesses an individual with happiness, material gains, and relationship success. The Shukra Dasha starts at the age of 25 years, and its duration lasts 20 years. However, the actual period and the results of Shukra Dasha vary depending on Venus's positioning in the birth chart.

Impact on a Life's Path

Venus's position in the birth chart significantly influences an individual's life path. A strong and well-placed Venus enhances their creativity, artistic abilities, and worldly gains. It brings in the potential for a healthy and harmonious relationship and a pleasant personality. However, a weak and poorly placed Venus can cause relationships, finances, and health issues, leading to a lack of creativity and disinterest in aesthetics.

As a planet in Vedic astrology, Venus holds great significance. Its placement in an individual's birth chart influences various aspects of life, such as love, relationships, creativity, and worldly gains. Understanding Venus and its symbolism helps navigate life's challenges and maximize the planet's favorable influence. Venus represents the beauty, charm, and luxury in the world around you, and understanding its role helps harness its full potential.

Saturn (Shani)

Shani, the Saturn Navagraha.
https://commons.wikimedia.org/wiki/File:Shani_graha.JPG

The universe is full of energy. The placement and movement of celestial bodies such as planets, stars, and asteroids significantly affect individuals' lives. Vedic astrology relies on accurately positioning these cosmic objects to study their influence on people's lives. One of the most important among these celestial bodies is Saturn, known as *Shani* in

Vedic astrology. The planet Saturn has great significance in Vedic culture and astrology. This section explains Saturn's mythological background and characteristics and explores its impact on an individual's life path.

Mythological Background

Saturn is known as Shani Dev, the son of Lord Surya or the Lord of Karma, who brings justice in Hindu mythology. He is known for his strict and disciplined demeanor and is often depicted as a dark or blue-skinned deity carrying a bow and arrow. According to legends, Lord Ganesha once cursed Shani Dev, which made him arrogant and aloof toward the world. Later, he was saved by Lord Hanuman and dedicated his life to serving Lord Hanuman.

Saturn's Significance in Vedic Culture and Astrology

Saturn symbolizes discipline, hard work, and karma in Vedic culture. In astrology, it represents the tenth house, which is directly associated with a person's career and professional life. Since Saturn is related to hard work, it is considered the "Taskmaster" planet, and its influence can cause delays and hardships in an individual's career. Saturn is the "Lord of Time," signifying longevity, maturity, and stability.

Characteristics and Symbolism

Saturn's attributes are discipline, hard work, and responsibility. It is associated with the air element and is considered a dry and cold planet. Saturn rules Capricorn and Aquarius in Vedic astrology. Its symbol is a "*Gada*," or mace, representing strength and masculinity. Its gemstone is Blue Sapphire, which is said to bring success, fame, and fortune to those who wear it. Saturn's impact on a person's chart gives groundedness and practicality to their approach to life.

Planetary Cycles and Periods

Saturn's cycles are among Vedic astrology's most essential and closely monitored. It takes about two and a half years to traverse one zodiac sign, so its cycle is known as "*Sade Sati*." The Sade Sati period is challenging, as Saturn's influence can bring obstacles and hardships. It can be a period of maturity and growth if an individual can withstand the trials it poses. Saturn has a 29-year cycle, known as its "return" or "Sade Saath," marking a significant turning point in a person's life.

Impact on a Life's Path

Saturn's influence on a person's chart is associated with discipline, hard work, and challenges. It brings tough periods but great rewards for those who can withstand its hardships. A strong Saturn in a chart signifies good career prospects, as it promotes discipline and perseverance in an individual's approach. It promotes success, wisdom, and longevity. Conversely, a weak Saturn brings obstacles in an individual's career and personal life. Appeasing Saturn by performing rituals and wearing its Blue Sapphire gemstone to mitigate its adverse effects is advised.

Saturn, or Shani, is a planet of contradictions. Its influence can bring challenges and obstacles, but it also promotes success, maturity, and discipline. The impact of Saturn on a person's chart is closely monitored in Vedic astrology, and it is known to reward those who endure its hardships. Wearing Saturn's gemstone, Blue Sapphire, and performing propitiatory rituals can help curb its adverse effects. Understanding Saturn's characteristics, symbolism, and cycles is essential to navigating its impact on a person's life path.

Planetary Aspects and Combinations

Astrology can potentially explain the universe's patterns and cosmic forces at work. It helps individuals gain insight into planetary combinations and their impact on a person's birth chart. The influences of planets are closely monitored to assess their effect on an individual's life path in Vedic astrology. When two or more planets form aspects in a birth chart, they create combinations known as "*yogas.*" The presence of these yogas in an individual's chart can bring great fortune or cause difficulties. Let's explore the planetary aspects and combinations of Navagrahas in Vedic astrology.

- **Sun:** The Sun is a fiery planet associated with vitality and courage. It is believed to be the source of all energy on Earth and represents leadership and authority. The Sun has a positive influence when placed in the first or tenth house. However, it can harm an individual's life when placed in the eighth or twelfth house.
- **Moon:** The Moon is a watery planet associated with emotions and intuition. It represents feminine energy and impacts an individual's mental and emotional health. The Moon can positively influence when placed in the fourth or sixth house. However, it can cause mental and emotional health issues when placed in the eighth or twelfth house.

- **Mars:** Mars is a fiery planet associated with aggression, courage, and physical strength. It represents masculine energy and impacts an individual's physical well-being. Mars can positively influence when placed in the first or eighth house. However, it can cause health issues in the reproductive system when placed in the seventh or twelfth house.
- **Mercury:** Mercury is an earthy planet associated with intelligence, communication, and logic. It represents analytical thinking and impacts an individual's mental prowess. Mercury has a positive influence when placed in the second or sixth house. However, it can cause communication problems when placed in the eighth or twelfth house.
- **Jupiter:** Jupiter is an airy planet associated with wisdom, prosperity, and spirituality. It represents the Guru or teacher and impacts an individual's knowledge and wealth. Jupiter has a positive influence when placed in the first or fifth house. However, its presence in the sixth or twelfth house can cause financial problems.
- **Venus:** Venus is a watery planet associated with love, beauty, and relationships. It represents harmony and peace and impacts an individual's personal life. Venus has a positive influence when placed in the first or fifth house. However, its presence in the sixth or twelfth house can cause conflicts in personal relationships.
- **Saturn:** Saturn is an airy planet associated with discipline, hard work, and karma. It represents the tenth house, directly associated with a person's career and professional life. As Saturn is related to hard work, it is considered the "Taskmaster" planet, and its influence can cause delays and hardships in an individual's career.

The Navagrahas profoundly impact an individual's life and can influence their physical, emotional, and mental well-being in Vedic astrology. It is essential to consult a Vedic astrologer to understand your horoscope's planetary aspects and combinations to lead a fulfilling and happy life. The Navagrahas represent the universe's forces, and by understanding and harnessing their energies, an individual can succeed in all aspects of life.

Chapter 3: Rahu: The North Lunar Node

The North Lunar Node is a fascinating topic that has intrigued astronomers and astrologers for centuries. This mystical point in the sky is vital in Hindu astrology, influencing an individual's destiny and personality. Rahu is often associated with deceit, illusion, and worldly desires, but it also has the power to achieve great success and fame. Its placement in a person's birth chart can reveal deep insights into their character and life path. Despite its mystical nature, astronomers have studied Rahu and noted its movements and effect on other celestial bodies.

Rahu remains an enigmatic part of the universe, and its influence on people's lives continues to inspire curiosity and wonder. This chapter further explores Rahu's symbolism, astrological significance, and connections with Ketu, the South Lunar Node. It explores the mythology associated with Rahu, its representations, and its qualities. This chapter examines why it is often seen as a malefic planet and its great potential by analyzing its astrological implications. Ultimately, this chapter provides a deeper understanding of Rahu's power and influence on people's lives.

Rahu.
https://commons.wikimedia.org/wiki/File:Rahu_graha.JPG

Rahu in Mythology

The role of Rahu in Hindu mythology is fascinating and intricate. This mysterious lunar node and its counterpart Ketu are known for their powerful influences on our life and destiny. This section explores Rahu's significance in mythology, including his symbolic representations, role as a cosmic trickster, and appearances in other myths. Whether you are familiar with Hindu mythology or not, this section will intrigue and enlighten you on the complexities of this celestial entity.

The Dragon's Head

In Hindu mythology, Rahu is known as the *Dragon's Head* or the *north lunar node* and was born from a fairy named Sinhika and demon king Viprachitti. In Hindu art, Rahu is depicted as a serpent with no body, swallowing the Sun or the Moon during eclipses. His appearance is often associated with darkness, chaos, and deception. According to popular belief, Rahu is an evil force, causing confusion and illusions. However, in some cultures, Rahu is seen as a powerful force representing transformation and spiritual awakening, encouraging people to break free from self-imposed limitations.

Cosmic Trickster

Rahu also plays the role of a cosmic trickster in Hindu mythology, weaving a web of deceit and illusions. He is known for his ability to disguise himself and manipulate circumstances to achieve his goals. However, Rahu's tricks are double-edged and can bring prosperity or misfortune, depending on a person's actions. The mythology suggests that Rahu's influence is most substantial during the eclipses when the Sun and the Moon align, and Rahu appears to devour them. Meditating and avoiding risky decisions during this time is advised.

Rahu's Role in Other Myths

Besides his legendary role as the Dragon's Head and the cosmic trickster, Rahu also appears in various Hindu myths. He is associated with the demon king Bali and the goddess Kali, representing ambition, power, and transformation. In one tale, Rahu disguises himself as a god to drink the divine nectar and gain immortality, but the Sun and the Moon expose him and cut off his head, which becomes the north lunar node. As a result, Rahu swears vengeance against them and causes eclipses to devour them. In other myths, Rahu is portrayed as a wise and knowledgeable sage who helps the gods fight demons.

Rahu's role in Hindu mythology is complex and multifaceted, representing malevolence and enlightenment. As a celestial entity, Rahu has a powerful influence on people's lives, guiding them toward spiritual growth or leading to deception. You can better understand this lunar node's significance in your life by exploring Rahu's symbolic representations, his role as a cosmic trickster, and his appearances in other myths. Honor Rahu's presence and use his energy to transcend your limitations and embrace transformation.

Symbolism of Rahu

The universe is filled with mysteries, and one of them is astrology. Astrology is more than just star signs; it's a tool for guidance, self-awareness, and self-improvement. Every planet and celestial body has a significant role in people's lives and offers valuable insights. Rahu is a shadowy planet crucial in Vedic astrology. This mysterious planet has a complex character and holds significant symbolism.

Ambition and Materialism

Rahu is considered a malefic planet, as it represents ambition and materialism. It symbolizes the desire for more, especially material possessions. It is associated with the "never enough" mentality and the pursuit of wealth and status. Rahu's influence can inspire individuals to pursue their goals with enthusiasm and determination. However, it can also make people greedy, selfish, and materialistic, often creating an illusion of success and happiness and making them chase unattainable dreams. The key is to balance ambition with spirituality and to focus on meaningful goals that align with your values.

Deception and Illusion

Another Rahu symbolism is deception and illusion. Rahu is the master of disguise, which can create a false sense of reality. It makes people blind to the truth and prone to delusions. Rahu's impact can manifest as self-deception, manipulation, and betrayal. Its energy can cause distrust and cynicism, creating discord between intentions and actions. The key is to develop awareness, learn to see things as they are – and practice honesty and transparency.

The Shadow Self

The most potent Rahu symbolism is the shadow self. Rahu represents people's deepest fears, hidden desires, and suppressed emotions. It symbolizes the subconscious mind and holds the key to self-discovery. Rahu's influence can create turmoil and force you to confront your shadows. Shadow work is challenging but essential for personal growth and wholeness. You can heal wounds, overcome fears, and transform lives by embracing your shadow self.

Rahu is a powerful planet with significant symbolism in astrology. Its influence can inspire individuals to achieve greatness and create an illusion of success and happiness. Understanding Rahu's symbolism helps people navigate its energy and use its power for great benefit. By balancing ambition with spiritual values, developing awareness, and embracing your shadow self, you can transform your life and reach your highest potential. Let this exploration of Rahu inspire you to deepen your astrological knowledge and embrace your path toward self-discovery.

Rahu's Connections and Differences with Ketu

Astrology is a fascinating topic that has intrigued people for centuries. It gives insight into personalities and a life path based on the position of the stars and planets at birth. Two specific planets known for their power and influence are Rahu and Ketu. These two planets, North Node and South Node, have a unique connection and difference impacting life significantly. This section explores the shared significance, contrasting qualities, and different impacts on life that Rahu and Ketu possess.

Shared Significance

Rahu and Ketu are planets often discussed concurrently in astrology. They share the same axis and have a karmic relationship, influencing people's lives more potently. Rahu is known for its power and ambition, while Ketu is known for its spiritual and mystical qualities. Together, they represent the balance between material wealth and spiritual enlightenment.

In Vedic astrology, Rahu and Ketu are the shadow planets, meaning they do not have a physical existence. It allows them to be more assertive when influencing an individual's life. They are transpersonal planets, meaning they impact entire generations rather than just one person, making them essential when studying social, political, or historical events.

Contrasting Qualities

Despite being connected, Rahu and Ketu have contrasting qualities, making them unique. Rahu is shadowy and represents materialistic tendencies, illusions, and worldly desires. It encourages people to seek material wealth and power, often leading them to make impulsive decisions with negative consequences. This planet is associated with gambling, addiction, and other vices.

In contrast, Ketu is known for its spiritual and mystical qualities. It is often associated with detachment, renunciation, and liberation. It encourages people to seek inner peace and spiritual enlightenment. This planet is associated with meditation, yoga, and other spiritual practices.

Different Impacts on Life

Rahu and Ketu's impact on life varies according to an individual's birth chart and planetary position. Rahu's influence is strong during its planetary periods, creating highs and lows in an individual's life. It can lead to sudden positive and negative changes and make people ambitious, motivated, and driven. Its energy can cause confusion, fear, and anxiety, leading to impulsive decisions and risky behavior.

Ketu's influence is milder and has a slower and steadier effect. It often provides a sense of detachment and encourages people to focus on their spiritual path. It brings introspection and contemplation, leading to self-realization and spiritual awakening.

Rahu and Ketu have connections and differences making them essential when studying astrology. They represent the balance between material wealth and spiritual enlightenment and powerfully influence an individual's life. While they share the same axis and have a karmic relationship, they possess contrasting qualities leading people to see that every coin has two sides. Rahu's power, ambition, and materialistic tendencies can enhance or crash your life. In contrast, Ketu's spiritual and mystical qualities can help individuals focus on their spiritual path to liberation and self-realization. Both planets are essential and must be studied in-depth to understand their impact on people's lives.

Rahu as a Malefic Planet

In Hindu astrology, the nine planets are regarded as divine forces that shape people's lives to a great extent. However, out of the nine, one planet, Rahu, is often considered malefic due to its negative influence on various aspects of life. Rahu is the north lunar node known for its potency in creating confusion and uncertainty. This section discusses the reasons behind Rahu's malefic nature, its adverse effects on individual lives, and how to neutralize them.

Reasons for Its Malefic Nature

Rahu's malefic nature is primarily due to its interaction with other celestial bodies. Astrologers believe that Rahu's energy is highly potent, and when it connects with other planets, it forms solid and life-altering patterns resulting in chaos. Its position in an individual's birth chart is crucial as it greatly influences their life path and experiences. Rahu is known for its affinity with materialistic gains and can cause people to pursue their desires relentlessly, often leading to dissatisfaction.

Negative Effects of Rahu

One of Rahu's most significant adverse effects is confusion and chaos in life. Due to its malefic nature, people with strong Rahu in their birth chart often struggle with identity and direction. They undergo various changes and transitions, causing distress and anxiety. Rahu's influence on people's health, relationships, and career is also evident. It can cause sudden upheavals, unexpected changes, and unfulfilled desires. Rahu is known to cause obstacles in spiritual growth.

Neutralizing Negative Effects

While Rahu is considered a malefic planet, it is not necessarily *all bad*. Its adverse effects can be neutralized, and its energy positively channeled. One way is to work on your spiritual growth and practice mindfulness. Meditation, yoga, and other spiritual practices are excellent for connecting with your inner self and combatting the confusion and chaos caused by Rahu. Another way is to work on self-discipline and set clear goals for yourself. You can avoid being disillusioned by endless desires by channeling your energy toward specific goals.

Another suggestion is to wear gemstones like hessonite or gomed, associated with Rahu. These gemstones absorb the negative energy generated by Rahu and offer the wearer protection from its malefic effects. Consult an astrologer to find the right gem for your birth chart. Lastly, acknowledging and embracing the energy and lessons Rahu offers is essential. Instead of avoiding it, work on integrating energy positively to reach new heights.

Rahu is a powerful celestial force that can potentially stir up chaos and confusion in an individual's life. However, its energy can be positively channeled by understanding its malefic nature and neutralizing its adverse effects. Ultimately, it is up to you to use Rahu's energy for betterment and growth. Turn it into a force of positivity and inner growth with effort, discipline, and awareness, leading you toward spiritual and material bliss.

Unleashing Rahu's Positive Potential

In Vedic astrology, Rahu is often demonized as a malefic planet that causes chaos, destruction, and negativity. However, Rahu possesses a strong positive potential that can be harnessed to instill progress, innovation, and growth. It all depends on how you channel its energy. This section explores the power of Rahu and how to use it for good.

Realizing the Power of Rahu

Rahu is known as the planet of desires, obsessions, and ambitions. It represents the material world and people's worldly desires. When placed positively in an individual's birth chart, Rahu can bestow tremendous creativity, intelligence, and the ability to think outside the box. Rahu's energy is intense and can help you break free from limiting beliefs and explore new avenues of growth. However, if you let your desires and obsessions take over, you could fall victim to addiction, greed, and self-destruction. For example, if you have a positive Rahu in your chart, it might seem like you have endless passion and drive. But to make the most of it, you must focus on your goals and avoid getting lost in temporary pleasures.

Using Rahu's Energy for Good

Rahu's energy can be directed toward productive and meaningful pursuits. You can use Rahu's power to innovate, create, and achieve greatness. For instance, if you have a positive Rahu in your chart, you can excel as an entrepreneur, inventor, or artist. You could develop a laser focus on your work, unafraid to take risks and experiment with new ideas. Rahu's energy is not only about material success; it can elevate consciousness and deepen spiritual practice. Use Rahu's power to break free from old patterns, release past traumas, and seek higher wisdom.

Balancing Rahu's Energy

To unleash Rahu's positive potential, you must balance its energy with its opposite planet, Ketu. Ketu represents spiritual detachment, inner wisdom, and non-attachment. When Ketu's energy is integrated with Rahu's, you can use Rahu's potential balanced and harmoniously. Ketu helps you remain grounded, reflective, and aligned with your higher purpose. Let go of material attachments, and find inner peace by cultivating your spiritual awareness.

Rahu is a powerful planet that can be harmful and beneficial. It all depends on how you harness its energy. By realizing Rahu's potential, using it for good, and balancing it with Ketu's energy, you can unleash your creative force and achieve your goals. Taking guidance from an experienced astrologer and remaining mindful of your desires and obsessions, you'll maximize Rahu's energy. Use this planet's energy wisely and transcend to new heights.

Astrological Benefits of Rahu

Imagine having the ability to enhance your career growth, bring peace and stability to your life, improve relationships, boost your confidence, and provide spiritual growth all at once. You can experience it precisely by understanding the astrological benefits of Rahu, the North Lunar Node. Rahu is one of the most powerful planets in the solar system, with a significant influence on people's lives. This section delves into Rahu's five most significant astrological benefits and how to harness them to transform your life.

Enhances Career Growth

Rahu is closely linked to fame and success, making it a wonderful planet to tap into for career growth. Rahu is associated with innovation, unconventional thinking, and ambition. Due to its unrelenting nature, Rahu energy can help you achieve remarkable progress in your career. When Rahu is favorable, it leads to excellent opportunities for career growth, promotions, and salary increases. By tapping into Rahu's positive energy, you can harness its potential to climb the ladder of success in your chosen field.

Peace and Stability

Rahu has a unique relationship with the Moon, and when placed in favorable houses, it can bring emotional stability and peace to an individual's life. When placed in the first, sixth, and eleventh houses, Rahu can bring about personal growth, intelligence, and success. This positive energy can help individuals feel more connected to their inner selves, leading to higher inner peace.

Improves Relationships

Rahu can impact relationships positively and negatively. It can bring about favorable terms with partners, enhancing the quality of relationships when placed in the seventh house and favorably positioned. Under Rahu's energy influence, people can experience profound understanding, cooperation, and support from their partners. When favorable in the horoscope, Rahu improves communication and smoother mutual understanding in relationships.

Boosts Confidence

Rahu is closely associated with self-confidence, personal power, and charisma. When Rahu favors individuals in their horoscopes, they feel more empowered and confident in all areas of their lives. Rahu can help individuals overcome their inhibitions, allowing them to take decisive and confident steps toward their goals. Rahu energy can give individuals the courage to make bold and unconventional decisions, aiding them in achieving their goals.

Provides Spiritual Growth

Rahu is not only about material success and fame. It also profoundly impacts spirituality and personal growth. Rahu's energy can bring about deep introspection and mystical experiences, leading to spiritual growth and enlightenment. Individuals develop spiritual awareness, leading to eliminating negative energies, thoughts, and habits when Rahu is placed in the eighth or twelfth house. Rahu's energy helps individuals better understand the universe and their place in it, leading to a spiritual awakening.

Rahu, the North Lunar Node, undoubtedly has a powerful and beneficial impact on people's lives. From career growth to personal growth, confidence building to relationship improvement, Rahu energy has many astrological benefits. However, Rahu's power can lead to harmful situations when unfavorably aligned. Therefore, working with skilled astrologers to understand how Rahu's energy interacts with your horoscope is critical. You'll harness the incredible potential of Rahu energy and experience tremendous benefits in all areas of your life.

Chapter 4: Ketu: The South Lunar Node

Ketu, known as the *South Lunar Node*, is a celestial body that has captured the attention of many throughout history. Ketu is a powerful force in the astrology realm that represents spiritual liberation and enlightenment. As the opposite point from Rahu, the North Lunar Node, Ketu is often associated with the past and release from Karma. Whether you believe in astrology or not, there's no denying the intrigue and mystique surrounding Ketu. Its energy and symbolism have inspired countless interpretations and analyses, making it a fascinating subject for seekers of knowledge.

This chapter provides an in-depth look at Ketu and its importance in Hindu mythology, Jyotish Shastra (Vedic Astrology), and other spiritual practices. Firstly, it briefly overviews Ketu in Hindu mythology, exploring the associated stories and legends and their role in Mahabharata. Then, it delves into the Ketu's symbolism, its role in astrology, and its effects on the 12 zodiac signs. Lastly, it discusses Ketu's negative and positive influences and a few remedies for overcoming its malefic effects.

Ketu.
https://commons.wikimedia.org/wiki/File:Ketu_graha.JPG

Ketu in Hindu Mythology

Hindu Mythology is full of fascinating stories and characters that have intrigued people for centuries. Among these characters is Ketu, a celestial body known as the *moon's south node*. Ketu is a peculiar planet as it doesn't have a physical existence, yet it holds immense importance in Hindu Astrology. This section explains Ketu's significance in Hindu Mythology and explores its legends and associated stories.

Legend of the Dragon's Tail

Ketu is often called the "Dragon's Tail" per Hindu Mythology. The legend behind the name has been passed down for generations. Once, during the churning of the ocean or the Samudra Manthan, a celestial being appeared and took the form of a dragon. This dragon is known as *Ketu*. The gods and demons churning the ocean were terrified of the dragon. Lord Vishnu's Sudarshan Chakra killed it. This scene is depicted in various Hindu art forms.

Role in Mahabharata

Ketu is also mentioned in the epic Mahabharata. During the Kurukshetra War, Ketu was the one who saved the Pandavas. Ketu was invisible to the Kauravas; therefore, it helped the Pandavas by secretly attacking their enemies. However, Arjuna, the warrior for the Pandavas, sensed Ketu's presence during the war and shot an arrow toward him. Lord Agni interfered and helped Ketu, which earned Arjuna a curse that he would never use his divine weapon again.

Samudra Manthan

Ketu is vital in Samudra Manthan, as the dragon reappears in this tale. During the churning of the ocean, a toxic poison was released, which could destroy the world. Lord Shiva drank the poison with immense power, and Ketu came to his aid. Due to Ketu, Lord Shiva's throat became blue, earning him the name *Neelkanth*.

Ketu's Astrological Traits

Ketu's importance is not limited to mythology; it holds great significance in astrology. According to Vedic astrology, Ketu is known as a shadow planet believed to harm a person's birth chart. Ketu represents things experienced, good or bad, in an individual's past life. It indicates the areas in a person's life they must focus on to grow and improve.

Ketu might be an invisible planet to the naked eye, but it is greatly important in Hindu Mythology. The associated stories and legends are intriguing and enriching simultaneously. From Samudra Manthan to the Kurukshetra War, Ketu has been profoundly significant. Its role in astrology makes it even more crucial as it shows people the areas they must improve in their lives. The Dragon's Tail will continue to fascinate people for generations.

Symbolism of Ketu

In Jyotish Shastra, Ketu is a well-known planet with deep spiritual significance. This spiritual planet has the power to liberate a person from the cycle of birth and death and make an individual transcend the materialistic world. A strong Ketu in an individual's astrological chart signifies spiritual orientation and deep insight into the universe's mysteries. This section dives into Ketu's mystical symbolism and unearths the profound significance of this planet in Jyotish Shastra.

Liberation from the Earthly Bondage

Ketu possesses the power to break the bond between an individual and the materialistic world. It helps people realize that all they see, do, and experience is temporary and perishable. Ketu awakens you to the fact that spiritual attainment is the ultimate goal of human life. A strong Ketu in an astrological chart signifies the person strives for spiritual growth, ultimately leading to liberation from the cycle of birth and death. Ketu also helps individuals gain supernatural powers and attain enlightenment.

Significance in Jyotish Shastra

In Jyotish Shastra, Ketu is linked with an individual's fate, spiritual growth, and enlightenment. The planet can enlighten you about past-life karma and its consequences in this lifetime. It represents mysticism, divination, and occult sciences. A person with a strong Ketu usually possesses unmatched intuition and psychic abilities. However, Ketu can bring negativity to an individual, leading to personal and professional life challenges. A strong Ketu in an individual's astrological chart can cause misfortunes and hardships.

Impact on Karma

Ketu impacts an individual's Karma, or actions and deeds. As an individual's soul moves from one life form to another, it carries the Karma from previous lives. Ketu signifies that an individual must detach from these Karmas to attain spiritual growth and enlightenment. It highlights the importance of living in the present while striving for the ultimate goal. A strong Ketu in an individual's astrological chart indicates the person is working toward karma detoxification and realizing the soul's true purpose.

Navigating Ketu's Influence

Ketu profoundly affects an individual's life with negative and positive influences. Individuals must incorporate spiritual practices to navigate the Ketu's impact, including meditation, introspection, and self-reflection. The path to spiritual growth and enlightenment requires sacrifice, patience, and conscious living. Individuals must avoid unethical and immoral practices that could worsen Ketu's impact.

Ketu represents spiritual growth, enlightenment, and liberation from the cycle of birth and death. It has immense significance in Jyotish Shastra and impacts Karma. The journey to spiritual growth is not easy, but a strong Ketu in an individual's astrological chart signifies the person is on the right path. Understanding Ketu's mystical symbolism is essential to navigating its influence positively. Incorporating spiritual practices and conscious living into your life can help you harness Ketu's transformative power.

Ketu's Role in Astrology

Astrology is an ancient practice many people still believe in today. One essential aspect of astrology that is often overlooked is Ketu, one of the nine planets in this system. Ketu is a unique planet, considered a benefic and malefic planet, depending on its placement and interaction with other planets. Understanding Ketu's role in astrology can provide insight into an individual's personality, relationships, and future. This section explores Ketu's importance in astrology, its effects on the twelve signs, and its malefic nature.

Ketu's influence on the twelve signs varies according to their placement in a person's birth chart. For example, if Ketu is in Aries, it will impact differently from when it is in Taurus or other signs. Ketu typically indicates spiritual growth and detachment, and people with solid Ketu placements in their birth chart are often drawn toward spirituality. It influences intuition and psychic abilities, guiding a person through life's experiences. Ketu in different signs affects the individual's personality traits.

Known for its malefic nature, Ketu can cause sudden changes, unexpected events, and accidents in an individual's life. It can worsen the effects of other malefic planets like Saturn and Mars. However, it should be remembered that its malefic nature is not constant but based on a person's astrological profile. For some people, Ketu might not have any harmful effects.

Ketu also has various parts of the day. It is considered Scorpio's diurnal ruler and Sagittarius's nocturnal ruler, meaning its influence was more potent during these periods. For example, if you are born during these periods and have strong Ketu placement in your birth chart, you'll feel the planet's impact more strongly.

Ketu has implications for relationships, especially romantic ones. It symbolizes unconventional and spiritual love not often understood by others because Ketu focuses on the spiritual path, which is different from what society considers the norm in relationships. Those whom Ketu influences in relationships are often content with solitude and don't require social validation. They prioritize spiritual growth over material gains and societal expectations.

Ketu is an essential player in astrology that people often overlook. Understanding Ketu's placement in your birth chart can lead to a better understanding of the self, relationships, and your spiritual path. Ketu's malefic and benefic effects are determined by its interaction with other planets and a person's astrological profile. By learning about Ketu's rulerships over different parts of the day and its impact on relationships, you can use this knowledge to make informed decisions.

Negative Influences of Ketu

Known as the *South Node*, Ketu is the planet generally associated with karmic lessons and spiritual growth. However, it has adverse effects that could disrupt your life in various ways. When overshadowing other planets, Ketu could bring unexpected setbacks, health issues, and emotional stress diminishing your ability to succeed. This section explores some critical negative impacts of the Ketu planet, including its adverse effect on health, disruptive impact on relationships, and obstacles to professional growth.

Adverse Effects on Health

Ketu has a notably negative influence when overshadowing the health planet, making people vulnerable to health issues and diseases. The impact could be mental health problems, such as depression, anxiety, addiction, or physical ailments, like chronic pain, allergies, and infections. When Ketu overshadows the planet associated with vitality, individuals might feel lethargic, lacking energy, and unmotivated to push forward. Therefore, keeping a close eye on your health is essential, as Ketu's negative influence could be hard to spot.

Disruptive Impact on Relationships

Ketu impacts relationships, particularly romantic ones. The disruptive influence of Ketu makes individuals emotionally distant, leading to a lack of trust, engagement, and ineffective communication in romantic relationships. It leads to issues such as misunderstandings, arguments, and breakups. Individuals might continuously be unable to connect with people or establish meaningful relationships. Ketu's influence can lead to loneliness and emotional turmoil, making it challenging to navigate life.

Obstacles to Professional Growth

Ketu can disrupt professional growth, making identifying opportunities that could benefit a person's career challenging. Ketu's negative impact could cause a lack of clarity in decision-making, preventing career advancements. Additionally, Ketu overshadows the planet associated with wealth, making a person unable to accumulate wealth or resources. Therefore, it's difficult investing or pursuing new career opportunities that might positively impact a person's financial wellbeing.

Individuals must pay attention to Ketu's negative influences. Its impact could manifest in various ways, such as adverse effects on health, disruptive impacts on relationships, and obstacles to professional growth. However, understanding Ketu's negative influences can help individuals to navigate life and make wiser decisions to overcome the planet's harmful effects. Seeking spiritual guidance, understanding self through self-reflection, and practicing self-care are practical ways individuals can combat Ketu's negative impact and live more fulfilling lives.

Positive Influences of Ketu

Ketu is one of the most misunderstood yet powerful planets in Vedic astrology. It is often called the "shadow planet" because it has no physical form and is only a mathematical point in the horoscope. However, Ketu's impact on life can be significant, bringing spiritual transformation, growth opportunities, and access to knowledge. This section explores Ketu's positive influences on people's lives and how you can harness its energy for your benefit.

Spiritual Transformation

Ketu is associated with spirituality, enlightenment, and liberation. It is the planet that helps you detach from materialism and seek a higher purpose in life. If Ketu is well placed in your horoscope, it can lead to significant spiritual transformation and growth. People with a strong Ketu influence could be strongly inclined toward meditation, yoga, and other spiritual practices. They might understand the world beyond what is visible to the naked eye.

Opportunities for Growth

Ketu is often seen as a planet of detachment and endings. However, it can present opportunities for growth and transformation. Ketu's energy can help you let go of your past and create space for new possibilities to emerge. You can break free from old patterns and beliefs that no longer serve you. For example, a strong Ketu placement in your horoscope can motivate you to quit a toxic job or relationship and pursue your true passions, helping you to find peace and contentment through a simple life.

Access to Knowledge

Ketu is known for its intuitive and psychic abilities. It is the planet that helps people access knowledge beyond what is taught in schools or textbooks. Ketu's energy can bring you closer to your inner wisdom and intuition, allowing you to tap into universal knowledge. People with a strong Ketu influence could have a natural gift for divination, astrology, healing, or other esoteric subjects. Ketu represents ancestral knowledge and spiritual inheritance. Therefore, connecting with Ketu's energy allows you to access your ancestors' wisdom and learn from their experiences.

Ketu can bring tremendous positive influences into your life if you learn to harness its energy. You can achieve spiritual growth, create opportunities for transformation, and access universal knowledge. However, Ketu's energy can be intense and challenging. Therefore, working with an experienced astrologer to guide you through the nuances of Ketu's influence is essential. Understanding and embracing Ketu's energy can unlock your full potential and lead a fulfilling life.

Ketu Remedies

An essential element of Vedic astrology is the position of celestial bodies, including the Sun, Moon, planets, and Nakshatras, in determining the fortunes of an individual. Ketu significantly influences an individual's life, representing spiritual enlightenment and liberation. However, an adverse alignment of Ketu in the birth chart can cause various problems, including financial issues, health problems, and instability in personal and professional life. This section explores the most effective Ketu remedies to help you combat the adverse effects of a challenging Ketu placement.

Worshipping Ketu Yantra

One of the most potent and effective remedies for Ketu is worshipping Ketu Yantra. A Yantra is a geometrical representation of a particular deity or planet, which generates cosmic energies and attracts positive forces. A Ketu Yantra should be placed in the northeast corner of the house or office, facing north. Lighting incense and a lamp while praying to the Ketu Yantra is best. Ketu Yantra worship can help alleviate the adverse effects of Ketu and provide peace of mind and spiritual enlightenment.

Fasting on Tuesdays

Tuesday is considered the day of Lord Hanuman, and fasting on Tuesdays can substantially benefit an individual affected by Ketu. When fasting on Tuesdays, eat only once, preferably during daylight hours. Fasting helps purify the body and the mind and introspection. During fasting, reading the Hanuman Chalisa and offering prayers to Lord Hanuman to seek his blessings to deal with Ketu's malefic effects is recommended.

Donating Mustard Oil

Another effective remedy for Ketu is donating mustard oil on Saturdays. Ketu is associated with Lord Ganesha, known for his fondness for oil. Therefore, donating mustard oil can significantly reduce Ketu's negative impact on a person's life. It is vital to offer the oil to a priest or donate it to a temple or a needy person. This gesture helps generate positive Karma and blesses the individual with significant benefits.

Offering Prayers to Lord Shiva

According to Vedic astrology, Lord Shiva is Ketu's ruling deity. Therefore, offering prayers and performing puja to Lord Shiva helps alleviate the adverse effects of Ketu. Recite the Mahamrityunjaya Mantra while performing the puja to seek blessings from Lord Shiva to neutralize Ketu's malefic effects.

Performing Pariharams

The last Ketu remedy you can undertake is to perform Pariharam, a ritual to appease a particular planet. A Vedic astrologer can guide an individual to perform the appropriate Pariharam based on their birth chart. These rituals involve performing specific puja, wearing a particular gemstone, or pilgrimaging a particular temple or sacred place. Pariharams are considered the most potent remedies for any planet since they involve direct communication with divine power.

Vedic astrology offers a range of remedies and solutions to help individuals deal with the malefic effects of a challenging Ketu placement. The remedies mentioned in this section can help you overcome obstacles and find peace, stability, and prosperity. However, it is crucial to seek the guidance of a Vedic astrologer to determine the most effective remedy for your specific case. You can attract positive energy, achieve spiritual growth, and live a fulfilling life with the proper remedies and approaches.

This chapter explored Ketu's mythology as a shadow planet associated with the dragon's tail and its role in Hindu astrology. It discussed how Ketu could bring tremendous positive influences on people's lives, such as spiritual growth, transformation opportunities, and knowledge access. It explored the most effective Ketu remedies, such as worshipping Ketu Yantra, observing fast on Tuesdays, donating mustard oil, offering prayers to Lord Shiva, and performing Pariharams. With the right approach and remedies, you can overcome the effects of a challenging Ketu placement and live a fulfilling life.

Chapter 5: The Lunar Nodes and the Nakshatras

The study of the lunar nodes and the Nakshatras is a fascinating journey into the mysteries of the universe. These celestial bodies hold the key to understanding the ancient wisdom and knowledge passed down through generations. With a confident and passionate approach, you can unlock the secrets of the lunar nodes and the Nakshatras and explore their connection to life. By discovering the meaning and power behind these celestial phenomena, you can gain insight into your true purpose and find balance and harmony within yourselves and the world around you.

This chapter provides an in-depth look at the Nakshatras, exploring their associations with specific deities, qualities, and characteristics and their relevance in predictive astrology. It explores the relationship between the lunar nodes and the Nakshatras, discussing how Rahu and Ketu influence the star they occupy. Lastly, this chapter guides how to use the Nakshatras for personal growth and development. So, dive into the wonders of the lunar nodes and the Nakshatras and embark on an incredible journey of self-discovery and enlightenment!

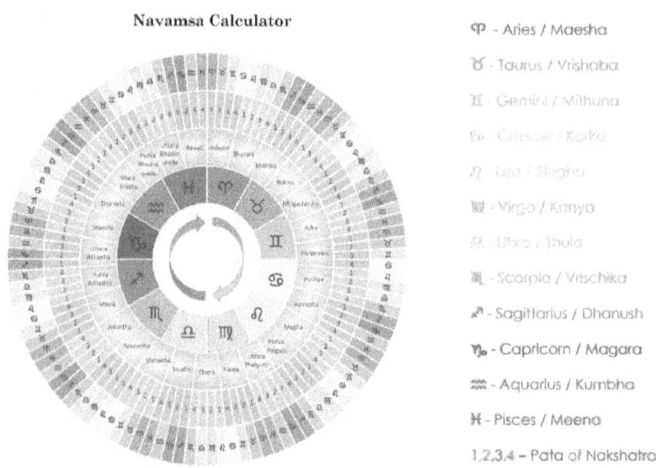

The Nakshatras are crucial in Vedic astrology, as they form the basis for determining horoscopes, planetary positions, and doshas or karmic imbalances.
Jaivanth, CC BY-SA 4.0 <https://creativecommons.org/licenses/by-sa/4.0>, via Wikimedia Commons
https://upload.wikimedia.org/wikipedia/commons/8/8a/Navamsa_calculator_by_using_pata_of_n akshatra_-_English_version.png

Understanding the Nakshatras

In Hindu astrology, Nakshatras or lunar mansions are important celestial bodies dividing the entire zodiac into 27 segments. Each Nakshatra possesses unique energy and symbolism, impacting individuals' lives in various ways. Understanding the Nakshatras is crucial for anyone interested in astrology or seeking insight into their destiny, personality, and life trajectory. This section comprehensively explores the essence of the Nakshatras, their association with deities, and the qualities and characteristics they bring to people's lives.

What Are the Nakshatras?

The Nakshatras are clusters of stars visible in the night sky. They correspond to the Moon's movement across the zodiac and are essential for calculating auspicious times for various activities like marriage, childbirth, and travel. Each Nakshatra occupies a span of 13 degrees and 20 minutes within a sign and is associated with a particular sound, symbol, and ruler. The Nakshatras are divided into three groups based on their fundamental characteristics or temperaments: fiery, earthy, and airy. Knowing your Nakshatra can help you understand your key strengths, vulnerabilities, and growth areas.

Associations with Deities

Each Nakshatra is associated with a particular deity, planetary influence, and element. Understanding these associations' properties helps you invoke your Nakshatra's energy and enhances your personal growth and spiritual evolution. For example, Ashwini, the first Nakshatra, is associated with the horse-headed twins of Vedic mythology, the Ashwini Kumaras, symbolizing healing and rejuvenation. Revati, the last Nakshatra, is associated with Lord Vishnu, the preserver of the universe, and blesses believers with spiritual liberation and fulfillment.

Qualities and Characteristics

The Nakshatras have unique qualities and characteristics impacting lives in numerous ways. For example, Rohini, the fourth Nakshatra, is associated with luxury, beauty, and sensuality and gives material prosperity and artistic talent to those born under it. Anuradha, the seventeenth Nakshatra, symbolizes loyalty, commitment, and deep emotional bonding and blesses believers with lasting relationships and social influence.

Impact on Vedic Astrology

The Nakshatras are crucial in Vedic astrology, as they form the basis for determining horoscopes, planetary positions, and doshas or karmic imbalances. Each Nakshatra has a unique planetary ruler, determining its impact on an individual's life path and destiny. For example, Punarvasu, the seventh Nakshatra, is ruled by Jupiter, the planet of wisdom and expansion, and blesses believers with prosperity, knowledge, and spiritual growth.

Application in Daily Life

Understanding the Nakshatras helps individuals navigate life's challenges, tap into their inherent genius, and make conscious decisions aligning with their divine purpose. Knowing your Nakshatra can identify your core strengths and improve your weaknesses. Use the divine energy of your Nakshatra to enhance your spiritual practices, cultivate deeper self-awareness, and align with your true nature. Whether you're a beginner or an advanced practitioner of Vedic astrology, the Nakshatras hold the key to a more prosperous, fulfilling life.

The Nakshatras offer a profound insight into the cosmos and your unique place. By understanding the essence of each Nakshatra, you can tap into your divine potential, harness the inherent gifts of your personality, and create a life aligned with your true destiny. Whether you seek material success, spiritual enlightenment, or emotional fulfillment, the Nakshatras provide a time-tested roadmap for navigating life's challenges and achieving your highest potential.

Types of Nakshatras

Nakshatras have been significantly relevant in Vedic astrology since ancient times. "Nakshatra" is derived from Sanskrit, meaning "a star." It refers to the positioning of the Moon in one of the 27 constellations or Nakshatras at birth. Each Nakshatra holds a unique significance, characteristics, and impact on an individual's life. This section discusses the three Nakshatras: Movable Nakshatras, Fixed Nakshatras, and Dual-Nature Nakshatras.

Movable Nakshatras

Movable Nakshatras are the first nine Nakshatras, from Ashwini to Ashlesha. These Nakshatras signify change, movement, and new beginnings. Individuals born under these Nakshatras are naturally inclined to make changes and seek new opportunities in life. They have a restless spirit and a desire for adventure. They are excellent leaders, risk-takers, and decision-makers. People with movable Nakshatras are usually rash, impulsive, and impatient.

Fixed Nakshatras

Fixed Nakshatras are the second nine Nakshatras, from Magha to Revati. These Nakshatras signify stability, permanence, and determination. Individuals born under these Nakshatras have strong willpower and are focused on achieving their goals. They are practical, disciplined, and patient. They are usually successful and wealthy. However, people with fixed Nakshatras can be stubborn and resistant to change. They can fall into a comfort zone and become rigid in their thinking.

Dual-Nature Nakshatras

Dual-Nature Nakshatras are the last nine Nakshatras, from Uttarashada to Abhijit. These Nakshatras signify characteristic blends of movable and fixed Nakshatras. Individuals born under these Nakshatras are adaptable, versatile, and balanced. They can move between being adventurous and practical according to the situation. They typically have excellent communication skills and are generally good at building relationships. However, people with dual-nature Nakshatras can be indecisive and need help sticking to a plan.

The Importance of Understanding Nakshatras

Understanding the Nakshatras can give insight into your natural tendencies, strengths, weaknesses, and life path. It helps individuals make better life decisions and understand the areas to improve. Astrologers use Nakshatras to analyze different aspects of a person's life – relationships, careers, finances, health, and more. Many Vedic astrology followers use Nakshatra-based remedies to overcome challenges and improve overall wellbeing.

Nakshatras are essential aspects of Vedic astrology, and understanding the different Nakshatras gives valuable insight into people's lives. Movable Nakshatras signify change and new beginnings, Fixed Nakshatras represent stability and determination, and Dual-Nature Nakshatras embody a blend of both. Knowing your Nakshatra can clarify your natural tendencies and help you to make better life decisions. In Vedic astrology, Nakshatras are a guiding light helping individuals lead happy, fulfilling lives.

Significance of Nakshatras

Each Nakshatra has unique characteristics, representing different strengths and weaknesses in an individual's life. They are described in various ancient texts such as Surya Siddhanta, Vedas, and Puranas, and are critical in Vedic astrology. However, their importance goes beyond astrology. This section delves into the Nakshatras' practical, astrological, and cultural significance.

Astrological Significance

Nakshatras influence an individual's personality traits, life events, and career paths. In Vedic astrology, each planet possesses its Nakshatra, which controls its effects in the horoscope. For instance, if the Moon is in the Rohini Nakshatra, it brings abundance, beauty, and fertility to an individual's life. If the Moon is in the Mula Nakshatra, it might bring loss, unrest, and challenges. Astrologers use Nakshatras to predict an individual's horoscope and guide them toward their destiny.

Practical Significance

Nakshatras have practical significance in many aspects of life. For instance, they determine the most auspicious time for performing rituals like weddings and naming ceremonies. Each Nakshatra influences the timing of events based on its qualities. Besides, they are used in

Ayurveda to determine the appropriate time to treat different ailments. The healing properties of the herbs and plants in Ayurveda vary depending on the Moon's position in the Nakshatra at harvest. The practical significance of the Nakshatras is evident in Indian martial arts, where the techniques are broken down and practiced according to the different Nakshatras.

Cultural Significance

Nakshatras are tightly interwoven into India's cultural fabric. They influence the naming of individuals - a person's Nakshatra is considered when choosing a name. Nakshatras represent the various deities and mythological characters in Hinduism. For instance, Krittika Nakshatra represents Agni, the god of fire, and is considered auspicious for performing fire-related rituals. In Hindu mythology, each Nakshatra has its stories and meanings and is considered sacred. The cultural significance of Nakshatras is evident in India's various festivals and rituals.

Nakshatras hold immense significance in Indian culture. They are prevalent in Vedic astrology, martial arts, Ayurveda, and other aspects of life. They represent the different deities in Hinduism and are essential in cultural rituals and festivals. Understanding the Nakshatras' significance helps people appreciate India's deep and rich cultural heritage.

Using Nakshatras in Predictive Astrology

Astrology has been around for ages, and for good reason. It is more than a pseudo-science or a way to identify personality traits. Astrology is a tool to guide people through life, help them make informed decisions, and better understand themselves and the world around them. Nakshatras are a vital aspect of astrology, often overlooked in Western astrology.

Nakshatras are lunar mansions in Hindu astrology and help determine a person's destiny, character, and life path. This section explores using the Nakshatras in predictive astrology to determine favorable and unfavorable periods, analyze current and future transits, and make accurate predictions.

Determining Favorable or Unfavorable Periods

The first way Nakshatras can be used in predictive astrology is by determining favorable and unfavorable periods by examining the Moon's placement in your birth chart and identifying its Nakshatra. Each Nakshatra has unique qualities and is associated with specific areas of life. For example, Rohini Nakshatra is associated with wealth, while Uttra Bhadrapada is associated with spirituality.

During unfavorable periods, you could experience obstacles or challenges related to the Nakshatra's qualities. Understanding the Nakshatra's qualities can prepare you for challenging times and make informed decisions accordingly. Similarly, during favorable periods, you could experience a streak of good luck or success in areas related to the Nakshatra. By pre-identifying these patterns, you can use them to your advantage.

Analyzing Current and Future Transits

The second way Nakshatras can be used in predictive astrology is by analyzing current and future transits. Transits are the planet's and celestial bodies' movements, impacting people's lives, like the planet's placement in your birth chart. Understanding the Nakshatras' qualities help you understand how current and future transits affect you.

For example, suppose a planet is transiting through a Nakshatra associated with obstacles. In that case, you must prepare emotionally and mentally to face challenges. Similarly, if the transit is through a Nakshatra associated with success and prosperity, expect a period of good luck, so take advantage.

Making Predictions Based on Nakshatras

The third way Nakshatras can be used in predictive astrology is by making accurate predictions. You can predict various aspects of life, like marriage, career, and health, by examining the Nakshatra placements in the birth chart and analyzing current and future transits.

For example, if a person's Moon is in the Magha Nakshatra, there could be a strong desire for recognition and fame. If a planet transits through this Nakshatra, there might be an opportunity for fame and glory. However, it could be challenging, as Magha Nakshatra can be associated with pride and arrogance.

Personal Development

The fourth way Nakshatras can be used in predictive astrology is as a tool for personal development. Understanding the qualities of the Nakshatras can help identify your strengths and weaknesses to improve yourselves. For example, if a person's Moon is in the Revati Nakshatra, they might be creative and empathic. However, they might struggle with indecisiveness and worry excessively. Knowing these qualities can help a person work on their decision-making skills and learn to manage their worries.

Nakshatras are powerful tools in predictive astrology, helping people understand themselves better, make informed decisions, and make accurate predictions. By using Nakshatras to determine favorable and unfavorable periods, analyzing current and future transits, making predictions based on Nakshatras, and using them for personal development, you can take charge of your life, navigating life's challenges with greater ease and clarity. So, if you're interested in exploring the world of astrology further, explore the Nakshatras and discover the many ways they can enhance your life.

The Relationship between the Nakshatras and the Lunar Nodes

The Nakshatras are used to create a sky map to determine the positions of the stars and planets. The Lunar Nodes, Rahu and Ketu, are shadow planets significantly impacting your lives. This section explores the relationship between the Nakshatras and the Lunar Nodes. It explains and provides examples of how Rahu and Ketu influence the Nakshatra they occupy.

Rahu's Influence on the Nakshatra It Occupies

Rahu is a malefic planet in Vedic astrology. It is associated with illusions, materialism, and darkness. When it occupies a Nakshatra, it can affect it in many ways. For instance, it can make the person born under that Nakshatra ambitious and materialistic or prone to temptations and addictions. Hence, Rahu is known as the planet of temptation.

Ketu's Influence on the Nakshatra It Occupies

On the other hand, the other shadow planet, Ketu, is associated with spiritual growth, liberation, and detachment. When it occupies a Nakshatra, it can make the person born under it detached, reserved, and spiritual. However, too much influence of Ketu on a Nakshatra can make the person anti-social, reserved, and withdrawn. Therefore, Ketu's placement in a Nakshatra is complex and must be analyzed carefully.

Examples of How the Lunar Nodes Affect Nakshatras

The Lunar Nodes are essential to people's lives because they are connected to karma and destiny. The position of the Lunar Nodes in a chart indicates challenges and lessons to be learned in this lifetime. Here are examples of how the Lunar Nodes influence the Nakshatras. If Rahu is placed in Krittika Nakshatra, it can make the person ambitious and power-hungry, leading to conflicts and challenges. If Ketu is placed in Revati Nakshatra, it can make the person spiritual and detached or anti-social and reserved.

The relationship between the Lunar Nodes and the Nakshatras is essential to Vedic astrology. The Lunar Nodes' position in a chart and the Nakshatras they occupy can indicate critical challenges, lessons, and opportunities in this lifetime. Therefore, understanding these shadow planets' impact on your lives and analyzing their placement carefully to make the most of them is essential.

Using Nakshatras in Your Life

Nakshatras, or birth stars, have been essential to Hindu astrology and Vedic culture for centuries. Specific constellations reveal important insight into your personality, strengths, and life challenges. By understanding your birth star and utilizing its unique energies, you can find greater harmony, balance, and fulfillment in all aspects of your life. This section explores the power of Nakshatras and how they can enhance your life.

Determining Your Birth Star

The first step is determining your birth star by knowing your time, date, and place of birth. With this information, you can use online calculators or consult an astrologer to discover your Nakshatra. Each Nakshatra has unique energies, ruling planets, and associated deities. Some Nakshatras are considered more favorable than others, depending on your specific birth chart and life circumstances. By understanding the qualities and characteristics of your Nakshatra, you gain valuable insight into your personality and life path.

Finding Compatible Partners

Another powerful way to use Nakshatras is to find compatible partners in love and marriage. Certain Nakshatras are considered more compatible with others in Vedic astrology based on their ruling planets and elemental qualities. By knowing your Nakshatra and potential partner, you can better understand your compatibility and potential challenges in a relationship. You can make more informed choices and build stronger, more harmonious relationships.

Enhancing Your Life with Nakshatras

Beyond love and relationships, Nakshatras can enhance various aspects of your life. Each Nakshatra is associated with different qualities and energies. By learning about them, you can tap into their power for more balance and harmony. For example, suppose you struggle with self-confidence or creative blocks. In that case, you can work with the Rohini Nakshatra energies associated with creativity, abundance, and sensuality. Work with the Uttara Phalguni Nakshatra energies, associated with peace, strength, and practicality, if you need more stability and grounding.

Making Personal Decisions with Nakshatras

Using the Nakshatras, you can make more informed decisions in your personal and professional life. Understanding the energies and qualities of different Nakshatras allows you to choose the best time and approach in various situations. For example, if you plan to start a new project or business, consult an astrologer to determine which Nakshatra is most favorable for beginning new ventures. If faced with a difficult decision or obstacle, meditate on the qualities of your birth star, and seek guidance from within.

Finding Strength in Your Birth Star

One of the most powerful ways to work with Nakshatras is to cultivate a deeper connection with your birth star. By understanding and embracing the qualities and energies associated with your Nakshatra, you can tap into your innate strengths and qualities. For example, if you were born under the Vishakha Nakshatra (associated with learning, exploration, and growth), you can focus on nurturing your natural curiosity and love for knowledge. Suppose you were born under the Purva Bhadrapada Nakshatra, associated with spirituality, intuition, and mysticism. In this case, explore practices like meditation, yoga, or spiritual teachings that align with these energies.

Nakshatra Meditation and Rituals

To fully embrace the power of Nakshatras in your life, incorporate meditation and ritual practices into your daily routine. Various Nakshatra-specific mantras, meditations, and offerings can help you connect with the energies and qualities of your birth star and find more balance and harmony. For example, perform a daily meditation where you visualize your birth star and its associated deity and focus on embodying its qualities. You could perform offerings or puja rituals to honor your birth star and seek its blessings in various areas.

Nakshatras are a powerful tool for self-discovery, growth, and transformation. By understanding your birth star and working with its unique energies, you can find more balance, harmony, and fulfillment. Whether you seek love, success, or inner peace, the Nakshatras can provide valuable insight and guidance to help you on your journey. So, learn about your birth star and explore the endless possibilities of this ancient Vedic wisdom.

Chapter 6: The Lunar Nodes in Birth Charts

The lunar nodes are a fascinating aspect to explore in birth charts. Each individual possesses a unique set of nodes, so the insights gained from analyzing them can be incredibly revealing. The North Node represents your soul's purpose and the path to fulfill it. The South Node indicates the traits and habits from past lives. By tapping into the energy of our planetary nodes, you can better understand your destiny and work toward aligning yourself with it.

This chapter aims to provide an in-depth look at the different placements of the lunar nodes in a birth chart. You'll apprehend their energies by examining their position relative to other planets, houses, and signs. Additionally, since transits to the nodes are thought to be incredibly potent, this chapter shows you how to calculate your nodal axis to track important dates. Whether you're a seasoned astrologer or just starting to dip your toes into birth chart analysis, the lunar nodes are a must-see. Get ready to be blown away by the wisdom they hold.

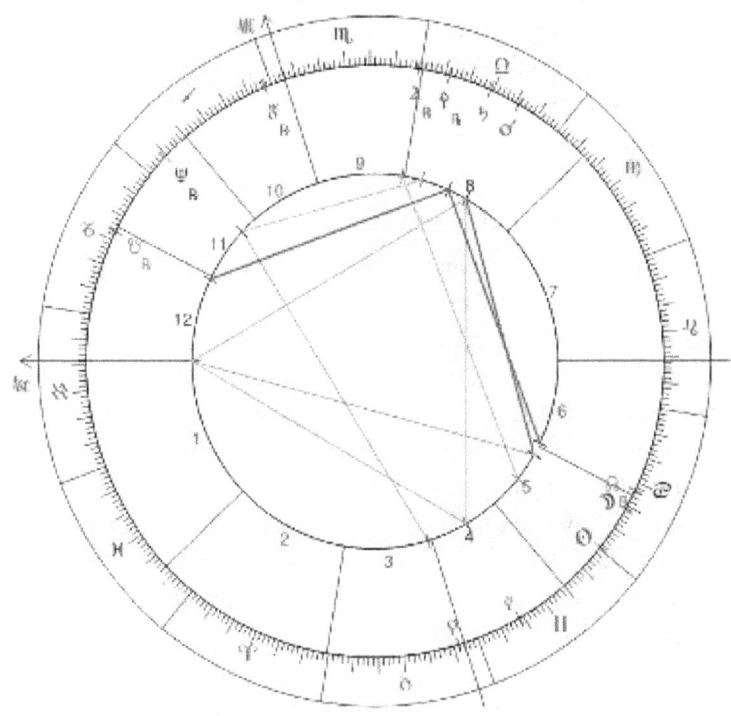

Sample birth chart.
Mom, CC BY-SA 3.0 <https://creativecommons.org/licenses/by-sa/3.0>, via Wikimedia Commons: https://commons.wikimedia.org/wiki/File:Natal_Chart_-_Adam.svg

Lunar Nodes Placements in a Birth Chart

Have you ever wondered what the lunar nodes in your birth chart mean? Some people overlook these celestial points, but they hold significant meaning and symbolism in astrology. The North Node and South Node represent your destiny and past lives, respectively. Understanding their placements can help you know your life purpose and evolution. This section delves into the lunar nodes' meaning, how to interpret their placements in your birth chart, and the effects of a nodal axis. Let's explore the mystical world of lunar nodes.

Understanding the Meaning of Lunar Nodes

Before interpreting the lunar nodes' placements, you must first understand their meaning. The North Node represents your future direction, soul mission, and growth potential in astrology. The South

Node symbolizes your past lives, talents, and karmic patterns. Together, these celestial points form a nodal axis revealing your life purpose and the areas requiring spiritual growth and transformation. While the North Node is associated with beneficial experiences, the South Node represents comfort zones that could hold you back from fulfilling your destiny.

Interpreting the North and South Node

Your birth chart must be calculated to know your North and South Node placements. The North Node and South Node positions are opposite, each falling in a specific astrological sign and house. The North Node's sign and house represent your potential new path, while the South Node's sign and house point to your past experiences and talents. For instance, if your North Node is in Aries and the 10th house, you might feel compelled to pursue an entrepreneurial career or leadership position in your field. Conversely, if your South Node is in Libra and the 4th house, you might struggle to balance your family life and career, as your past life experiences prioritize harmony and peace.

Analyzing the Effects of a Nodal Axis

When the North Node and South Node placements form a nodal axis, you experience periods of growth and challenges linked to your destiny and past lives. A nodal return (when the transiting North Node reaches your natal North Node's position) can be a pivotal time of self-discovery, spiritual awakening, and transformation. It's when you feel a pull toward new interests, people, and opportunities aligning with your life purpose. However, a nodal opposition (when the transiting North Node opposes the natal South Node) can cause internal conflicts, fears, and challenges blocking your spiritual growth. You must confront your past-life baggage and relinquish old patterns holding you back during these times.

Exploring Transits to the Nodes

The transiting planets affect your lunar nodes, triggering events and lessons aligning with your nodal axis. When the planet conjuncts or squares your North or South Node, it activates the nodal axis, bringing opportunities or challenges aligning with your destiny and past lives. For example, when transiting Pluto squares your natal North Node, you might experience a profound shift in your career or life path aligning with your soul's mission. But when transiting Saturn opposes your natal South Node, you could face obstacles and limitations related to your past-life patterns.

Calculating Your Nodal Axis

Calculating your nodal axis is easy. You can generate your birth chart for free online or consult an astrologer for an in-depth analysis. However, interpreting your nodal axis requires self-reflection and spiritual awareness. Understanding that your North Node isn't a quick-fix solution to your life challenges but a lifelong quest toward purpose and fulfillment is essential. You can align with your highest potential and manifest your dreams by embracing your soul's mission and releasing your past baggage.

The lunar nodes' placements in your birth chart carry valuable insight and symbolism into your soul's purpose and evolution. You can better understand your life journey and spiritual path by understanding the meaning of lunar nodes, interpreting their placements, analyzing their effects, exploring their transits, and calculating your nodal axis. The nodal axis represents a journey toward spiritual growth, awareness, and purpose. May you embrace your soul's calling and fulfill your destiny.

Lunar Nodes and Other Planets

Lunar Nodes are the points where the Moon's orbit intersects with the Earth's orbit around the Sun. The Lunar Nodes, the North Node and South Node, are essential in astrology as they represent the karmic energies from your past lives and your destiny in this lifetime. This section explores how the Lunar Nodes interact with the planets and how their conjunctions, transits, and aspects affect your life and natal chart.

1. **Sun:** When the Lunar Nodes align with the Sun, it can indicate a time of destiny and purpose in people's lives. The North Node is associated with your life path and the South Node with past karma. A conjunction between the North Node and the Sun can signify growth and development, while a conjunction between the South Node and the Sun can represent releasing of old patterns or habits. A transit of the North Node over the Sun in your natal chart is considered an important time of manifestation and success. In contrast, a transit of the South Node over the Sun can indicate letting go of ego and worldly desires.

2. **Moon:** As the Lunar Nodes are directly connected to the Moon's orbit, they strongly influence emotions and the subconscious. A conjunction between the North Node and the Moon can

represent emotional growth and spiritual development. It can also bring new connections and essential relationships. On the other hand, a conjunction between the South Node and the Moon can represent emotional healing and letting go of past hurts and traumas. A transit of the North Node over the Moon can bring emotional fulfillment and growth, while a transit of the South Node over the Moon can bring repressed emotions or detachment.

3. **Mercury:** As the planet of communication, Mercury has a solid connection to the Lunar Nodes. A conjunction between the North Node and Mercury can indicate intellectual growth and communication success. It can also bring new ideas and opportunities. A conjunction between the South Node and Mercury can represent revisiting old ideas or communication patterns needing release. A transit of the North Node over Mercury can bring intellectual breakthroughs and success in communication. In contrast, a transit of the South Node over Mercury can bring communication challenges or letting go of certain beliefs.

4. **Venus:** As the planet of love and relationships, Venus is strongly connected to the Lunar Nodes. A conjunction between the North Node and Venus can indicate romantic fulfillment and new relationships. It can also bring financial abundance and artistic success. A conjunction between the South Node and Venus can release old relationship patterns or financial habits. A transit of the North Node over Venus can bring new love and economic opportunities, while a transit of the South Node over Venus can bring challenges in love or financial losses.

5. **Mars:** As the planet of action and motivation, Mars has a solid connection to the Lunar Nodes. A conjunction between the North Node and Mars can indicate inspiration and drive toward your life purpose and goals. It can also bring new opportunities for leadership and success. A conjunction between the South Node and Mars can release old frustrations or anger patterns holding you back. A transit of the North Node over Mars can bring success in career and personal goals, while a transit of the South Node over Mars can bring challenges in motivation and energy.

6. **Jupiter:** Jupiter represents expansion, optimism, and growth. When in conjunction with the lunar nodes, it amplifies the North Node's effects, providing an opportunity for spiritual and personal growth. The transit of Jupiter over the nodal axis can signal significant progress and success. Similarly, the sextile or trine of Jupiter with the natal nodes can bring good fortune and abundance. However, if Jupiter is in square or opposition to the nodes, it can indicate excess, overindulgence, and a lack of restraint.
7. **Saturn:** Saturn represents discipline, responsibility, and limitations. It amplifies the South Node's effects in conjunction with the lunar nodes, promoting introspection, organization, and self-discipline. The transit of Saturn over the nodal axis can signal significant challenge and growth. Similarly, the sextile or trine of Saturn with the natal nodes can bring increased purpose and responsibility. However, if Saturn is in square or opposition to the nodes, it can indicate self-doubt, fear, and a lack of confidence.
8. **Uranus:** Uranus represents change, innovation, and independence. It amplifies the North Node's effects when in conjunction with the lunar nodes, providing an opportunity for radical transformation and self-discovery. The transit of Uranus over the nodal axis can signal significant upheaval and unpredictability. Similarly, the sextile or trine of Uranus with the natal nodes can bring sudden breakthroughs and insights. However, suppose Uranus is in square or opposition to the nodes. In that case, it can indicate rebellion, restlessness, and a lack of stability.
9. **Neptune:** Neptune represents spirituality, creativity, and illusion. It amplifies the South Node's effects in conjunction with the lunar nodes, promoting introspection, artistic expression, and emotional healing. The transit of Neptune over the nodal axis signals significant spiritual growth and connection. Similarly, the sextile or trine of Neptune with the natal nodes can bring increased intuition and empathy. However, if Neptune is in square or opposition to the nodes, it can indicate confusion, delusion, and emotional instability.

10. **Pluto:** Pluto represents transformation, power, and regeneration. It amplifies the North Node's effects when in conjunction with the lunar nodes, providing an opportunity for profound transformation and rebirth. The transit of Pluto over the nodal axis signals significant crisis and renewal. Similarly, the sextile or trine of Pluto with the natal nodes can bring intense personal growth and empowerment. However, if Pluto is in square or opposition to the nodes, it can indicate manipulation, obsession, and control.

In astrology, studying planetary placements is essential for gaining insights into people's lives, including your destiny, soul mission, and karmic lessons. Lunar nodes provide unique insight into spiritual and personal growth, particularly when examining their relationship with other planets. You can gain greater clarity and awareness of your life path and destiny by understanding how Jupiter, Saturn, Uranus, Neptune, and Pluto interact with the lunar nodes.

Lunar Nodes and Houses

Astrology has always intrigued people since time immemorial. The science of astrology originated thousands of years ago. This science is based on certain planetary positions influencing human behavior, thought, and actions. One crucial planetary position is the lunar nodes. The lunar nodes, or the North and South nodes, are calculated by taking the intersection point of the Moon's orbit and the ecliptic. In astrology, lunar nodes are significant in understanding karma, life purpose, and soul growth. This section explores the lunar nodes concerning the houses.

1. **First House:** The North Node in the first house signifies new beginnings, self-discovery, and self-expression. This placement indicates that individuals must focus on their individuality, take risks, and trust their instincts. The south node in the first house signifies that individuals must release their dependency on others and their ego and focus more on developing their personality.
2. **Second House:** The North Node in the second house signifies financial stability, self-worth, and security. This placement indicates that individuals must create stable groundwork and material prosperity. The south node in the second house signifies that individuals must release materialistic tendencies and

hoarding and concentrate more on spiritual growth.
3. **Third House:** The North Node in the third house signifies communication, networking, and learning. This placement indicates that individuals must focus on developing communication skills, connecting with people, and pursuing knowledge. The south node in the third house signifies that individuals must release their fear of speaking and dullness in learning and focus more on intellectual exploration.
4. **Fourth House**: The North Node in the fourth house signifies emotional wellness, rootedness, and family. This placement indicates that individuals must develop intuition, build emotional connections, and create a supportive home environment. The south node in the fourth house signifies that individuals must release past family traumas and emotional instability and focus more on creating their identity.
5. **Fifth House:** The North Node in the fifth house signifies creativity, self-expression, and romance. This placement indicates that individuals must focus on harnessing their creativity, pursuing their passions, and enjoying the pleasures of life. The south node in the fifth house signifies that individuals must release their tendency to rely on others for validation and superficial relationships and focus more on developing their unique talents.
6. **Sixth House:** The North Node in the sixth house signifies service, discipline, and health. This placement indicates that individuals must focus on caring for their physical and mental health, practicing self-discipline, and contributing to society through service. The south node in the sixth house signifies that individuals must release the workaholic, over-analyzing, and focus more on being in the present moment.
7. **Seventh House**: The North Node in the seventh house signifies partnerships, harmony, and diplomacy. This placement indicates that individuals must build healthy relationships, develop social skills, and practice compromise. The south node in the seventh house signifies that individuals must release their overly dependent on relationships and confrontational and focus more on developing self-reliance.

8. **Eighth House:** The North Node in the eighth house signifies transformation, depth, and intuition. This placement indicates that individuals must explore their hidden potential, embrace change, and develop their psychic abilities and sensitivity. The south node in the eighth house signifies that individuals must release the fear of change and secretiveness and focus more on living a life of transparency.
9. **Ninth House:** The North Node in the ninth house signifies spiritual quests, higher knowledge, and global awareness. This placement indicates that individuals must focus on exploring different cultures, pursuing higher education, and discovering their life purpose. The south node in the ninth house signifies that individuals must release dogmatic beliefs and rigid thinking patterns and focus more on exploring different perspectives.
10. **Tenth House:** The North Node in the tenth house signifies success, reputation, and ambition. This placement indicates that individuals must focus on achieving their goals, building a solid reputation, and leaving a legacy. The south node in the tenth house signifies that individuals must release their obsessive tendencies and fear of failure and focus more on balancing work and personal life.
11. **Eleventh House:** The North Node in the eleventh house signifies community, humanitarian pursuits, and social justice. This placement indicates that individuals must focus on social networking, contributing to social causes, and building a supportive community. The south node in the eleventh house signifies that individuals must release their tendency to isolate themselves, detach from emotions, and focus more on nurturing their relationships.
12. **Twelfth House:** The North Node in the twelfth house signifies spiritual awakening, solitude, and compassion. This placement indicates that individuals must focus on exploring their inner realm, practicing meditation, and developing empathy for others. The south node in the twelfth house signifies that individuals must release their addiction to escapism and self-pity and focus more on building their inner strength.

Lunar node position is an essential aspect of astrology, and understanding its relation to houses can help individuals know their life purpose, soul growth, and karma. Each lunar node placement has a unique representation. You can better understand its strengths, weaknesses, and potential growth areas by analyzing it. With this knowledge, individuals can navigate their lives with greater clarity, wisdom, and purpose.

Lunar Nodes and Signs

Astrology's influence on life cannot be denied, and one of its most exciting aspects is the study of nodes. Nodes are points in the sky where the Moon's orbit intersects with the ecliptic, significantly impacting your life. This section explores nodes concerning the signs, specifically looking at conjunctions, transits, aspects, and representation for each placement.

1. **Aries:** For those with a node in Aries, the focus is on individuality, impulsivity, and leadership. Conjunctions between a planet and the node can enhance these characteristics, whereas challenging aspects bring out negative qualities like selfishness or aggression. During transit, there could be opportunities for self-discovery and taking risks.
2. **Taurus**: With a node in Taurus, the focus is on material comfort, stability, and relationships. Conjunctions can bring out a sensual side, while challenging aspects can lead to materialism and stubbornness. There might be opportunities for financial gain or strengthening relationships during transit.
3. **Gemini:** With a node in Gemini, there is a focus on communication, learning, and adaptability. Conjunctions can enhance these qualities, while challenging aspects can lead to indecisiveness or superficiality. During transit, there could be opportunities for networking or expanding knowledge.
4. **Cancer:** Those with a node in Cancer focus on emotional security, nurturing, and intuition. Conjunctions can enhance these qualities, while challenging aspects can lead to moodiness or clinginess. During transit, there could be opportunities for healing and connecting with inner emotions.
5. **Leo:** With a node in Leo, there is a focus on creativity, self-expression, and leadership. Conjunctions can enhance these qualities, while challenging aspects can lead to arrogance or attention-seeking behavior. During transit, there could be

opportunities for self-discovery and creative endeavors.

6. **Virgo:** Those with a node in Virgo focus on practicality, organization, and service. Conjunctions can enhance these qualities, while challenging aspects can lead to perfectionism or criticism. During transit, there could be opportunities for improving health or career goals.

7. **Libra:** With a node in Libra, there is a focus on partnership, diplomacy, and aesthetics. Conjunctions can enhance these qualities, while challenging aspects can lead to indecisiveness or conflict avoidance. During transit, there could be opportunities for relationship growth or developing artistic talents.

8. **Scorpio:** Those with a node in Scorpio focus on transformation, intensity, and sexuality. Conjunctions can enhance these qualities, while challenging aspects can lead to obsession or power struggles. There could be opportunities for deep healing or exploring taboo topics during transit.

9. **Sagittarius:** With a node in Sagittarius, the focus is on expansion, philosophy, and adventure. Conjunctions can enhance these qualities, while challenging aspects can lead to restlessness or overindulgence. During transit, there could be opportunities for travel or spiritual growth.

10. **Capricorn:** Those with a node in Capricorn focus on ambition, responsibility, and tradition. Conjunctions can enhance these qualities, while challenging aspects can lead to pessimism or workaholic behavior. During transit, there could be opportunities for career advancement or stepping into a leadership role.

11. **Aquarius:** With a node in Aquarius, the focus is on innovation, individuality, and social justice. Conjunctions can enhance these qualities, while challenging aspects can lead to rebelliousness or detachment. There could be opportunities for social activism or exploring unique perspectives during transit.

12. **Pisces**: Those with a node in Pisces focus on spirituality, intuition, and creativity. Conjunctions can enhance these qualities, while challenging aspects can lead to escapism or emotional instability. There could be opportunities for emotional healing or connecting with higher powers during transit.

Nodes are significant in astrology, and understanding their placement of the signs offers valuable insight into people's lives. Conjunctions, transits, and aspects enhance or challenge the qualities associated with each placement, and focusing on these influences leads to personal growth and discovery. By exploring the nodes concerning the signs, you can deepen your understanding of yourself and harness the power of the cosmos.

Chapter 7: Karmic Patterns

Karmic patterns are deeply ingrained in people's lives, shaping experiences and influencing the future. Each decision sets into motion a series of events that can have a far-reaching impact. Some of these patterns are positive, helping individuals live their best lives, while others are harmful, leading to pain and suffering. But the beauty of karmic patterns is that you have the power to change them, break free from negative cycles, and manifest your desires. You can control your destiny and create a brighter future by being aware of your thoughts and actions.

This chapter explores karma and karmic patterns, how they are identified in a birth chart, and strategies for spiritual growth and overcoming karmic challenges. It discusses free will in karmic destiny and how to draw on past life knowledge to guide the present. The information will help you understand how karmic patterns influence your lives and empower you to make conscious choices fostering growth and fulfillment. With this knowledge, you can move forward in your spiritual journey with clarity and conviction.

A karmic pattern in which a woman gives a gift, and then receives one.
By Copyrighted to Himalayan Academy Publications, Kapaa, Kauai, Hawaii, CC BY-SA 2.5, via Wikimedia Commons: https://commons.wikimedia.org/w/index.php?curid=1857404

Karma and Karmic Patterns

Karma is a universal law governing people's lives. Your thoughts, feelings, and actions in this life shape your destiny in the next. A karmic pattern is a recurring event or pattern in your life that can be traced back to decisions or actions from a previous life. Understanding karma and karmic patterns can help you navigate life and make better choices for your future. This section explores karma, how karmic patterns work, and how the Moon's lunar nodes shape your destiny.

What Is Karma?

Karma is rooted in Hindu, Buddhist, and Jain beliefs. Your actions, thoughts, and intentions in this life have consequences that determine your future. If you do good deeds, you'll be rewarded with good karma and punished with bad karma if you do bad deeds. Karma is not a punishment but a natural consequence of a person's actions, which could transcend multiple lifetimes.

How Karmic Patterns Work

Karmic patterns are repetitive behaviors or events in your current life linked to previous lifetimes. For example, it could be a karmic pattern if you are constantly in volatile relationships or have a recurring health issue. When you do not learn the lessons from past lives, these patterns repeat until you correct your behavior. Recognizing and changing these patterns is the key to breaking the cycle and improving your life.

Lunar Nodes and Karma

The Moon's nodes are positioned in the Moon's orbit where it crosses the ecliptic. The North and South nodes are points forming an axis in astrology and influence a person's destiny. The North Node represents a person's goals and karmic destiny, while the South Node represents past lives and lessons. Placing these lunar nodes in your natal chart informs you about your karmic destiny and how you can learn from your past lives.

Understanding karma and karmic patterns helps you make better life decisions and work toward a positive future. You can break free from the cycle of negative behaviors and experiences by recognizing and correcting your habits. Knowing your lunar node placements provides insight into your karmic patterns and how to work toward your life goals. Remember, karma should not be feared but rather to learn and grow. Control your destiny and create a positive future through self-awareness and self-improvement.

Identifying Karmic Patterns in a Birth Chart

Birth charts are the blueprint of people's lives in astrology. It indicates the position of the stars and planets at birth. This information lets astrologers read your personality traits, strengths, weaknesses, and karmic patterns. Karma is your actions and decisions in the past influencing your future. The cycle of action and reaction is a continuous process affecting a person's life. This section explains how astrology can analyze karma and help you identify the karmic patterns in your birth chart.

Understanding How Astrology Can Analyze Karma

The study of astrology propounds that karma is the driving force behind people's lives. It helps you understand your life's positive and negative patterns and how they relate to your soul's evolutionary journeys. Astrologers believe karma manifests in different forms and is reflected in the birth chart. Each planet, sign, and house in the birth chart signifies various aspects of karma. For example, Saturn's position in a birth chart represents karma from past lives, so when faced with struggles and obstacles, it is often linked with Saturn's placement in the chart.

Charting the Karmic Pattern

Astrologers look for patterns indicating a karmic influence when analyzing a birth chart. One essential karma indicator in the birth chart is the South Node or Ketu's position. The South Node represents the karma from past lives. The North Node or Rahu represents your karmic destiny. The South Node's position in any of the twelve astrological signs shows the nature of the challenges a person will likely face in this lifetime. For instance, if the South Node is in Aries, the person might face assertiveness and anger management challenges.

Exploring Life Lessons and Past-Life Karma

Each planet in the birth chart influences karma differently. For example, Venus's placement signifies the love you give and receive, while Mars's position indicates physical energy and determination. The Moon represents your emotional state and how you handle emotions. An astrologer can identify the karmic lesson you need to learn in this lifetime by analyzing these planets' placements. Whether related to love, compassion, courage, or honesty, these lessons help a person grow spiritually and overcome past-life karma.

A birth chart is essential for identifying karmic patterns and providing insight into your soul's path. Understanding the planet's position, astrological signs, and houses in the chart can help clarify your life journey and how it relates to your past-life karma. You can overcome karmic challenges by making conscious decisions, working on spiritual growth, and focusing on the lessons to be learned. With the help of an astrologer and the insight of your birth chart, you can understand yourself deeper and create a brighter future.

Overcoming Karmic Challenges

Karma has been around for ages and is significant in people's lives. The universal principle of cause and effect dictates that every action has an equal and opposite reaction. Karmic challenges are the consequences of your actions and choices you must face in this life or the future. Overcoming these can be difficult, but it's essential for spiritual growth. This section explores various ways to overcome karmic challenges and achieve spiritual growth.

Dharma: Its Role in Spiritual Growth

Dharma is the path toward enlightenment and fulfillment. Fulfilling your dharma is essential to spiritual growth and overcoming karmic challenges. Your dharma is specific to you. It's your life's purpose and unique qualities. You can overcome karmic challenges by fulfilling your dharma and harmonizing with it. However, you must understand your dharma and your role in life to achieve spiritual growth.

Self-Awareness and Reflection

Self-reflection is awareness of your actions, thoughts, and emotions, crucial for spiritual growth. Self-awareness helps identify the areas you must improve and make the necessary changes. You must reflect on your experiences and learn from them. When you take responsibility for your actions, you learn from your mistakes, leading to spiritual growth. Self-awareness and reflection are essential for recognizing karmic patterns, allowing you to break free from them.

Practicing Karma Yoga

Karma Yoga is the yoga of action, offering your actions to the divine without expectations of reward or fruit. This practice keeps you detached from your actions' outcomes and focuses on doing your duty without attachment or judgment. When performing actions with detachment, you create positive karma, reducing negative karmic challenges. Practicing Karma Yoga helps overcome ego and develop an understanding of service to humanity, a crucial aspect of spiritual growth.

Forgiveness

Forgiveness is a powerful tool for spiritual growth and overcoming karmic challenges. When you forgive others, you release negative emotions like anger, resentment, and bitterness, freeing yourself from karmic patterns. Forgiveness does not mean forgetting what happened. Rather it's about letting go of negative emotions and moving forward. You can achieve self-growth by forgiving yourself for your mistakes. By forgiving others, you create positive karma instead of negative patterns.

Mindfulness

Mindfulness is the practice of being present and fully engaged at the moment. It is aware of your thoughts, emotions, and actions without judgment. Mindfulness allows you to connect with your higher self and access inner peace, transcending karmic challenges. When you live mindfully, you notice the beauty around you and appreciate every moment of life - practice mindfulness daily to promote spiritual growth and overcome karmic challenges.

Overcoming karmic challenges is essential to your spiritual journey, requiring dedication and effort. You can move beyond past karmic patterns and achieve spiritual growth by understanding your dharma, practicing self-awareness and reflection, and performing Karma Yoga, forgiveness, and mindfulness. Remember, every challenge is an opportunity for growth and learning. It's up to you to make the best of it. With these practices, you can create a better future, free from negative karmic patterns, and achieve spiritual growth.

Strategies for Working with Karmic Patterns in Life

Have you ever felt trapped by repetitive situations in life that seem to have no end? Do you sometimes feel stuck in negative cycles and can't break free? These recurring patterns are karmic patterns. Everyone has karmic patterns they must overcome, but they can be challenging, especially without the right strategies. This section explores some tips on working with karmic patterns and turning them into opportunities for growth and self-discovery.

Approaching Difficult Situations with Compassion

One of the best ways to work with karmic patterns is to approach difficult situations compassionately. You'll see things differently when approaching a difficult situation with an empathetic and understanding mindset. Compassion allows you to see the problem for what it is and helps you release anger or resentment. Only then can then move forward with practical steps to resolve the situation. Practicing self-care and taking time for yourself is important to promote compassion. The more you do this, the better equipped you are to face karmic patterns with compassion.

Recognizing Karmic Patterns in Your Life

The first step to transforming your karmic patterns is recognizing them. Reflect on your life and examine negative situations or behaviors that keep repeating. You can take responsibility for your karmic patterns and let them go when you realize them. Journaling and meditation are helpful tools. Further, explore your karmic patterns by looking into a birth chart analysis. It gives insight into the deeper karma associated with your life and how it affects you.

Setting Intentions to Move Forward

Setting intentions is an effective way to shift the energy in a situation. Identify the behavior or problem you want to change, then set your intention. Write down your choice and place it where you can see it daily. This regular reminder helps you stay focused and motivated to achieve your goal. Setting intentions releases you from your karmic patterns and gives you the power to create something new and move forward into a brighter future.

Connecting with Resources for Further Support

You don't have to work with karmic patterns on your own. Connect with resources and support to help you stay on track. It could be a therapist, coach, or a trusted friend or family member who can provide emotional support and guidance. Only you can decide what's best for you. However, having a support source is invaluable in transforming your karmic patterns. Use all the resources available to improve yourself and find inner peace.

Incorporating Mindfulness into Your Acts and Thoughts

Mindfulness is being present and fully engaged at the moment. Incorporating mindfulness into your daily life makes you more aware of your actions and thoughts. You'll make conscious choices to break free from negative patterns and create new, positive ones aligning with your goals. Mindfulness helps cultivate acceptance and compassion, offering connectedness with the world around you.

Practicing Gratitude

Practicing gratitude is a powerful tool for transforming karmic patterns. When focusing on what you're grateful for, you shift your energy into a positive state. Take time each day to reflect on what you're thankful for, regardless of how small it seems. This practice releases negative energy and helps you move forward with a positive mindset. If you struggle to find things to be grateful for, look around and appreciate the little things in life. There is beauty all around; it's up to you to recognize it.

Karmic patterns are challenging and sometimes overwhelming, but they don't have to control your life. You can transform karmic patterns into opportunities for growth and self-discovery by approaching situations with compassion, recognizing patterns, setting intentions, connecting with resources, incorporating mindfulness, and practicing gratitude. Remember, this journey is not a quick fix, but with consistent effort and self-reflection, you can break free from negative cycles and find peace in your life.

Finding Balance in the Universe with Karma

Have you ever had a situation where it seems everything is going wrong? Your day might start with a flat tire on the way to work, and then you spill coffee on your shirt as soon as you arrive. It's easy to feel like the universe conspires against you in those moments. But what if there was a way to find balance, even amid the chaos? Enter karma. Karma is a concept that has been around for centuries and helps people understand the interconnectedness of all things.

Achieving Harmony through Understanding Karma

Karma is the concept that actions have consequences, positive or negative. It's often associated with "what goes around comes around." If you do good things, good things will happen. If you do bad things, bad things will happen. But karma is much more complex than that. It's not just a matter of cause and effect. It's about achieving harmony in the universe. When you understand that everything you do impacts the world around you, you'll act in a way promoting balance and harmony.

Recognizing the Interconnectedness of All Things

Actions don't exist in a vacuum; they impact the people and the world around you. You'll see the world differently when you recognize karma's interconnectedness and understand that your actions have a ripple effect. If you do something good for someone else, that person might do something good for someone else. It's a chain reaction that can positively impact the world.

Learning from Your Karmic Experiences to Grow Spiritually

Karma isn't only about the repercussions of your actions. It's about the lessons you learn from experiences. When you experience something positive or negative, it's an opportunity for growth. You learn from your mistakes and use the knowledge to make better choices in the future. It's not always easy to see the lesson at the moment, but with time and reflection, you understand yourself and the world better.

Practicing Karma in Everyday Life

Practicing karma in everyday life is about being aware of your actions and their impact on the world. It's about doing good for others without expecting anything in return. It's about treating others with kindness and respect. It's about taking responsibility for your mistakes and making amends. It's not always easy to do these things, but the more you practice, the more natural it becomes.

Finding balance in the universe with karma is about understanding that your actions have consequences, recognizing the interconnectedness of all things, and learning from your experiences. Practicing karma in your everyday life creates a positive ripple effect, profoundly impacting the world. It's not always easy to stay mindful of your actions and their impact, but the more you practice, the more you create a balanced and harmonious world. So, the next time you're having a bad day, remember everything you do has an impact, and focus on doing good for yourself and others. The universe will thank you.

Unlock Your Karmic Potential with Birth Chart Insight

Astrology is an ancient practice to gain insights into personalities, relationships, and the future. But did you know astrology can provide insight into past lives? By analyzing your birth chart, you can unlock your karmic potential and better understand the lessons to learn in this lifetime. This section explores using astrology to analyze karma, incorporating the lunar nodes into your birth chart analysis, and taking action to unlock your karma's potential.

Using Astrology to Analyze Karma

The moon's South Node represents karma in your birth chart in astrology. The South Node represents the lessons and experiences you have mastered in past lives. It describes the patterns and behaviors you might repeat in this lifetime. By analyzing the placement of the South Node in your birth chart, you gain insight into the areas where you might be stuck or must break free from old patterns. For example, if your South Node is in Taurus, you could struggle with attachment to material possessions. By recognizing this pattern, you can let go of your attachment to material things and focus on cultivating inner wealth.

Incorporating the Lunar Nodes into Your Birth Chart Analysis

In addition to the South Node, your birth chart includes the North Node. The North Node represents the life lessons you must learn in this lifetime. For instance, the areas of your life you feel challenged or uncomfortable but where growth and evolution are possible. By analyzing the placement of the North Node in your birth chart, you gain insight into your purpose in this lifetime. For example, suppose your North Node is in Sagittarius. In that case, you should embrace adventure, explore new horizons, and open your mind to new ideas.

Taking Action to Unlock the Potential of Your Karma

Once you have gained insight into your past lives and purpose in this lifetime, it's time to take action to unlock your karma's potential. It involves various practices, such as meditation, journaling, or working with a therapist. It includes developing new habits or routines. For example, you might benefit from daily mindfulness meditation if you struggle with anxiety. Or, if you struggle with self-esteem, you'll benefit from practicing affirmations or other self-care practices. By taking action to break free from old patterns and cultivate new habits, you unlock your karma's potential and move toward a more fulfilling and joyful life.

Astrology is a powerful tool for unlocking your karmic potential and gaining insight into your purpose in this lifetime. Analyzing the placement of the lunar nodes in your birth chart gives you insight into your past lives and life lessons in this lifetime. Breaking free from old patterns and cultivating new habits, you unlock your karma's possibilities and move forward to a more fulfilling and joyful life. Why not give astrology a try? Who knows what insights you might learn about yourself and your future?

The Role of Free Will in Karmic Destiny

It's a fundamental human desire to control your life and shape your destiny. But how much control do you have? Karma suggests that your actions in past lives dictate your present circumstances. So, where does free will happen? Are you merely a puppet in the grand scheme of things, or can you actively choose your path? This section dissects the intersection of destiny and free will and how understanding this relationship can help guide you toward your ultimate purpose.

Determining Your Fate

Karmic destiny suggests that past life actions predetermine certain events and circumstances in your current life. However, this doesn't mean you are powerless to shape your future. Every decision made in the present creates a ripple effect impacting your future. You have a specific path to follow, but it's up to you to decide how to navigate it and what you learn from it. It's like a choose-your-own-adventure book. The outcome might be set, but how you travel toward that outcome is entirely up to you.

Understanding the Intersection of Destiny and Free Will

There is a delicate balance between destiny and free will. Fate sets the framework for life, while free will allows you to make choices impacting the outcome of that destiny. Free will choices have positive and negative consequences shaping your karmic future. For example, if you continuously act selfishly and harm others, you'll likely experience adverse effects. Conversely, making choices that benefit others and contribute positively to the world makes you more likely to experience positive outcomes.

Drawing on Past-Life Knowledge to Guide Your Present

Typically, a person does not remember their past lives, but you can draw on the wisdom and knowledge gained from them to guide the present. You might have an innate skill or talent you can't explain or a strong urge to pursue a specific career or path. These could be manifestations of past-life experiences and knowledge guiding you toward your ultimate purpose. By tapping into this knowledge, you better understand yourself and your path and make choices aligned with your karmic destiny.

Embracing the Uniqueness of Each Individual's Path

Lastly, knowing that each individual's path is unique, despite the overarching frameworks of karmic destiny and free will, is essential. You might have similar experiences or encounter similar obstacles, but your reactions and choices ultimately shape your paths. It is tempting to compare your progress to others or try to follow someone else's path, but this ultimately undermines your growth and progress. You can thrive and fulfill your ultimate purpose by embracing your individuality and making choices aligning with your karmic destiny.

Karmic destiny and free will can be daunting. How can you balance these seemingly opposing forces to create your best life? Ultimately, it's about understanding that you have agency, even navigating predetermined frameworks. You comprehend your path and purpose by making choices aligning with your karmic destiny and drawing on past-life knowledge. You'll thrive on your unique journey by embracing your individuality and avoiding comparing others. So, control your choices and embrace the often-mysterious intersection of destiny and free will.

Chapter 8: Remedies for Malefic Rahu and Ketu

Rahu and Ketu are two of the most powerful planets in Vedic astrology - those who feel their impact know how intense their influence can be. Representing the lunar nodes, these two planets are notorious for causing disruptions and chaos in people's life. However, you can harness their power for positive change by understanding their energy and functioning. Rather than fearing these planets, use their transformative energy to propel yourself forward. It's all about perspective and learning to work with cosmic forces.

This chapter in the Vedic astrology journey provides remedies for mitigating the adverse effects of malefic Rahu and Ketu. These remedies must be used with sincerity and faith and should not be considered a substitute for professional advice or medical treatment. With the right attitude and approach, these remedies can be powerful tools for growth and prosperity. So, embrace the challenge and see the amazing things you can accomplish under Rahu and Ketu's influence.

Lord Ganesha.
Niranjan Arminius, CC BY-SA 4.0 <https://creativecommons.org/licenses/by-sa/4.0>, via Wikimedia Commons: https://commons.wikimedia.org/wiki/File:Lord_Ganesha_cropped.jpg

Worshipping Lord Ganesha

In Hindu astrology, malefic Rahu and Ketu are often associated with adverse effects on an individual's life, such as financial troubles, health problems, and relationship issues. However, a remedy for these malefic planets has been suggested since ancient times - worshipping Lord Ganesha. Hinduism's elephant-headed god removes obstacles and provides prosperity and success in life. This section explores how you can worship Lord Ganesha to help alleviate malefic Rahu's and Ketu's adverse effects.

Offering Prayers to Lord Ganesha

This is one of the easiest and most effective ways to seek his blessings. Begin your day praying to Lord Ganesha and seeking his guidance and blessings. You can light a lamp and incense sticks and offer flowers and fruits to Lord Ganesha to show your devotion. A simple prayer to Lord Ganesha can be chanted 108 times daily or recited in the famous Shri Ganapati Atharva Shirsha Mantra.

Reciting the "Om Gan Ganapataye Namaha" Mantra

Chanting the "Om Gan Ganapataye Namaha" mantra is a powerful way to invoke Lord Ganesha's blessings. This mantra removes obstacles and brings success and happiness. Recite this mantra 108 times a day for 21 days, and you'll see positive changes in your life. If you cannot chant it 108 times daily, you can recite it 11 or 21 times.

Participating in Ganesh Chaturthi Celebrations

Ganesh Chaturthi is a famous festival celebrated throughout India in honor of Lord Ganesha. Participating in these celebrations can powerfully connect with Lord Ganesha and seek his blessings. Many people create beautiful idols of Lord Ganesha at home and perform the puja to mark the occasion. The festivals are usually full of fun and joy; the energy can help ward off negative influences in your life.

Creating a Home Shrine for Lord Ganesha

Creating a home shrine for Lord Ganesha is excellent for developing a personal relationship with the deity. Place an image or idol of Lord Ganesha in your home and offer prayers to him daily. You can light a lamp, offer flowers and fruits, and recite the "Om Gan Ganapataye Namaha" mantra to invoke Lord Ganesha's blessings. The shrine's energy helps ward off negative influences and attracts positive energies.

Visiting Local Ganesh Temples

Visiting local Ganesh temples is another way to connect with Lord Ganesha and seek his blessings. Many temples have specific days for worshipping Lord Ganesha, like Tuesdays and Chaturthi days. Visit the temple during these auspicious days and offer prayers to Lord Ganesha to remove obstacles in your life. From time to time, take part in a local Ganesh festival that the temple celebrates and absorb the positive energy of devotion.

Worshipping Lord Ganesha is a powerful remedy for malefic Rahu and Ketu. It removes obstacles and brings prosperity and success. By offering prayers, chanting the "Om Gan Ganapataye Namaha" mantra, participating in Ganesh Chaturthi celebrations, creating a home shrine, or visiting Ganesh temples, you can seek Lord Ganesha's blessings and alleviate the adverse effects of malefic Rahu and Ketu. So, start worshipping Lord Ganesha today and attract prosperity and success.

Chanting Rahu and Ketu Mantras

When Rahu and Ketu are in an unfavorable position, they can create chaos, confusion, and uncertainty. Fortunately, some remedies mitigate their adverse effects. One remedy involves chanting specific mantras for Rahu and Ketu. This section explores some effective mantras and rituals to help balance these malefic planets and improve your life.

Chanting the Mahamrityunjaya Mantra

The Mahamrityunjaya mantra is powerful in Hinduism and is said to conquer death. This mantra is effective in balancing malefic Rahu and Ketu. Chanting this mantra helps remove obstacles, reduces anxiety, and promotes overall wellbeing. The mantra goes like this: Om Tryambakam Yajamahe, Sugandhim Pushti Vardhanam, Urvarukamiva Bandhanan, Mrityor Mukshiya Maamritat.

Performing Abhishekams with Coconut Water

Offering coconut water to Rahu and Ketu is a traditional and effective remedy for balancing these planets. The water has a cooling effect on the hot and fiery nature of the malefic planets. Performing this Abhishekam on Tuesdays or Saturdays is recommended for maximum benefit. The ritual involves making a hole in a coconut and pouring water with flowers into it, simultaneously offering your prayers to Rahu and Ketu.

Offering Red Flowers to Rahu and Ketu

Red is associated with Rahu and Ketu, so offering red flowers to these planets is a common and effective remedy. Red flowers like hibiscus, roses, and lotus can calm the malefic energies of these planets. It can improve relationships, bring business success, and promote stability and security. To perform the ritual, hold a red flower, offer your prayers to Rahu and Ketu, and place the flower toward these planets.

Chanting the "Om Bhraam Bhreem Bhroum Sah Rahave Namah" Mantra

Another powerful mantra for balancing Rahu is the "Om Bhraam Bhreem Bhroum Sah Rahave Namah" mantra. This mantra helps remove obstacles and negativity caused by Rahu and promotes peace and harmony. Chanting this mantra 108 times on Saturdays is recommended for maximum benefit. In addition, you can chant the "Om Shraam Shreem Shroum Sah Ketave Namah" mantra to appease Ketu.

Lighting a Lamp with Sesame Oil on Saturdays

Lighting a lamp with sesame oil on Saturdays helps balance Rahu and Ketu. Lighting a lamp in front of a picture or statue of Rahu and Ketu and offering prayers is recommended. The sesame oil lamp absorbs these planets' negative energies and promotes positive energy. Performing this ritual on Saturdays for maximum benefit is advised.

Malefic Rahu and Ketu can create chaos, uncertainty, and obstacles. However, some remedies help mitigate their adverse effects. Chanting specific mantras, performing Abhishekams, offering red flowers, and lighting a lamp with sesame oil are a few of the most effective remedies. You can achieve balance, stability, and success by incorporating these remedies into your spiritual and daily life. These remedies are not meant to replace medical or psychological support but can complement and enhance your overall wellbeing.

Donating Black Items

The positioning of planets in your horoscope significantly shapes your life's events. When Rahu and Ketu are in a malefic position, it can cause various problems like financial troubles, health issues, relationship problems, and more. However, one prominent remedy to counter these inauspicious effects is to donate black items. This section discusses the different black things you can contribute to appease Rahu and Ketu.

- **Donating Black Clothes:** One of the simplest ways to appease Rahu and Ketu is by donating black clothes. Dasharatha, Rama's father, presented black clothes to Lord Rama and his brothers to ward off the ill effects of Rahu and Ketu during the Sani-Sadhe-Satti period. You can donate black dresses to the underprivileged, especially during an Amavasya, to mitigate Rahu and Ketu's negative energy.

- **Donating Black Sesame Seeds:** Another way to nullify Rahu and Ketu's adverse impact is by donating black sesame seeds. In Hindu mythology, Lord Vishnu applied black sesame seeds to his body, helping him attain his legendary color and bestowing him with the power to conquer enemies. You can seek Rahu and Ketu's blessings by donating black sesame seeds

to a poor person or a pious Brahmin.
- **Donating Black Gram:** Black Gram or "*Urad Dal*" is another item you can contribute to appease Rahu and Ketu. Donating Black Gram (a South Asian legume) on Saturdays and Amavasya days, in Lord Shani's name, helps reduce these planets' inauspicious effects. You can donate it to the underprivileged to ward off the negative impact of Rahu and Ketu.
- **Donating Charity in Lord Shiva's Name:** Performing charity in Lord Shiva's name is one of the most potent remedies to counter malefic Rahu and Ketu effects. Donating to the poor and needy in the name of Lord Shiva helps calm Rahu and Ketu's energy, reducing their negativity toward the person. Charities can be done by visiting Shiva temples and distributing prasadam (holy food) to the devotees.
- **Making Donations to Needy Families on Amavasya:** The significance of donating to needy families on Amavasya is undervalued. During the no-moon night, Rahu and Ketu's energy is at maximum, allowing individuals to seek their blessings through various charities. You can donate items like black clothes, sesame seeds, or black gram to low-income families lacking necessities.

Donating black items is one of the powerful remedies to counter the malefic effects of Rahu and Ketu. By donating black clothes, sesame seeds, and black gram, performing charity in Lord Shiva's name, and making donations to needy families, you can mitigate the malefic energy of these planets. However, seeking the guidance of an experienced astrologer before performing a remedy is recommended.

Wearing Gemstones Associated with Rahu and Ketu

Astrology has always been the guiding light for those who believe celestial bodies significantly impact human lives. The belief is that planets in certain favorable or opposing positions influence people's lives positively or negatively. According to Vedic astrology, Rahu and Ketu create chaos, confusion, and negativity in a person's life. However, the good news is that wearing certain gemstones associated with Rahu and Ketu can help alleviate their harmful effects. This section delves further into which gems can help you ward off the malefic effects of Rahu and Ketu.

- **Wearing Hessonite Garnet (Gomed):** Gomed is a beautiful stone belonging to the grossularite mineral group. It is known as the *Cinnamon Stone* and is a brownish-orange to orange-red color. Hindu astrologers believe that Hessonite, or Gomed, is the gemstone to balance the malefic effects of Rahu. Wearing a Hessonite garnet will help combat the negative aspects of Rahu, like financial loss and difficulties with worldliness, material goods, and victory over enemies.
- **Wearing Cat's Eye (Lehsunia):** Another gemstone associated with Ketu is the Cat's Eye (Lehsunia). The natural Cat's Eye stone is a member of the Chrysoberyl mineral family. Cat's Eye is considered positive for those affected by Ketu and brings good fortune and health. It helps ward off negative vibrations, promotes spirituality, and provides balance.
- **Getting Gemstones Astrologically Approved Before Use:** Consulting an expert astrologer specializing in gem recommendations is crucial before acquiring a gemstone. Based on your astrological chart and doshas, an expert will determine if the rock would be best for you. The wrong gemstone can do more damage than good. Hence, getting them approved by an expert astrologer is always essential.
- **Wearing the Gemstones on the Appropriate Day:** Wearing them on the appropriate day is essential, enhancing the rock's effects. Wednesday, Thursday, and Friday are the auspicious days to wear Hessonite and Cat's Eye.

Rahu and Ketu are two malefic planets impacting a person's life in numerous undesirable ways. However, wearing the right gemstone can help you alleviate the adverse effects of these planets. Hessonite Garnet (Gomed) and Cat's Eye (Lehsunia) are the two gemstones known to balance Rahu and Ketu's impact. But consulting an expert astrologer before wearing a gemstone is crucial. A good astrologer will help you determine which rock is best based on your astrological readings. Wearing the jewel on the right day is essential for optimum benefits. Therefore, wearing the right gemstone can bring about positive changes and help you combat the adverse effects of Rahu and Ketu.

Performing Puja

The idea of malefic Rahu and Ketu can be daunting. Known as the shadow planets in Vedic astrology, they are associated with several challenges greatly influencing people's lives. Challenges can manifest in health issues, career setbacks, financial struggles, and personal relationships. However, with the right approach to dealing with these malefic planets, it is possible to find peace, prosperity, and success.

This section is dedicated to exploring the various methods of mitigating the adverse effects of malefic Rahu and Ketu. Whether offering prayers, performing pujas, or consulting with expert priests, you can harness the power of these shadow planets and overcome their obstacles in numerous ways. So, let us dive into the different aspects of remedying malefic Rahu and Ketu.

Offering Prayers to Rahu and Ketu

Prayer is one of the simplest and most effective ways to mitigate the malefic effects of Rahu and Ketu. Reciting specific mantras and stotras dedicated to these shadow planets can appease their negative influence and gain blessings. Some of the commonly used mantras for Rahu and Ketu are:

- **Om Rahuve Namaha:** This mantra is dedicated to Rahu and should be chanted 18,000 times over 40 days to overcome the malefic effects.
- **Om Ketave Namaha:** This mantra is dedicated to Ketu and should be chanted 7,000 times over 21 days to overcome its malefic effects.

Offering Flowers and Incense to Rahu and Ketu

Another way to appease Rahu and Ketu is by offering flowers and incense. This ritual, known as *"pushpanjali,"* can be performed during Rahu or Ketu Kaal on Saturdays, Tuesdays, and Sundays. Offering red flowers and lighting incense sticks, you gain Rahu and Ketu's blessings and alleviate their adverse effects. The ritual can be completed by circling the offerings around the idols of these planets seven times and chanting mantras dedicated to them.

Participating in Pujas and Homas for Rahu and Ketu

Participating in pujas and homas dedicated to Rahu and Ketu is another effective way to overcome their malefic effects. These rituals involve worshipping specific deities associated with Rahu and Ketu, such as Lord Shiva, goddess Durga, and Lord Ganesha. By participating in these pujas, you can seek their blessings and gain protection from the negative influence of Rahu and Ketu. The rituals involve chanting mantras, offering flowers and incense, and engaging in puja. Some commonly used pujas for Rahu and Ketu are Ganesh Puja, Lakshmi Puja, and Mahamrityunjay Puja.

Performing Fire Rituals for Rahu and Ketu on Amavasya

Performing fire rituals or "havans" on Amavasya or the New Moon Day is another powerful way to appease Rahu and Ketu. By completing this ritual, you gain the blessings of the fire god, Agni, and alleviate the malefic effects of these shadow planets. The havan involves chanting specific mantras and offering ghee, honey, and other sacred materials into a fire. When completed with dedication and sincerity, the havan can positively change a person's life.

Consulting an Expert Priest before Performing Pujas and Homas

While the methods listed above are effective, consulting an expert priest before performing pujas and homas is essential. These rituals involve specific mantras, offerings, and procedures requiring proper guidance and supervision. A reputable priest with expertise in astrology and Vedic rituals will guide you in the right direction and ensure the remedies are performed correctly. A knowledgeable priest will help you determine your situation's best pujas and homas. Consulting an expert before undertaking a remedy ensures the rituals are done correctly and you gain the maximum benefits.

Dealing with malefic Rahu and Ketu can be challenging, but it's not an obstacle that can't be overcome. The abovementioned remedies can appease these shadow planets and mitigate their adverse effects. These remedies require consistency and patience. You must keep going even if you do not see immediate results. You'll find peace, prosperity, and success with a little effort and perseverance. A combination of dedication and prayers will bring the desired results.

Chapter 9: Navagraha Worship and Remedies

The Navagrahas, or the nine planets, hold tremendous power and influence over people's lives. From shaping successes and failures to impacting health and relationships, they profoundly affect who and what you become. Hence, Navagraha worship and remedies have gained popularity over the years. Offering prayers to these celestial bodies and adopting specific remedies mitigates the adverse effects of the planets and unlocks their positive potential. While the planets can pose challenges, they also provide opportunities for growth and prosperity.

This chapter provides a comprehensive list of Navagraha worship, rituals, and remedies to tap into the power of the planets and positively change your life. It includes tips and results of Navagraha worship to help you make the most of this practice. With dedication and faith, you can navigate the path of life easily and gracefully, guided by the divine Navagrahas' energy. You'll find the courage to face your challenges and have faith that everything will be all right. May you always find guidance, wisdom, and peace in the presence of the Navagrahas.

A woman worshipping the Navagrahas.
Ravindraboopathi, CC BY-SA 3.0 <https://creativecommons.org/licenses/by-sa/3.0>, via Wikimedia Commons: https://commons.wikimedia.org/wiki/File:Devotee_praying.jpeg

Navagrahas Rituals

In Hinduism, Navagrahas are considered significant cosmic forces influencing people's lives. Each rules over a specific aspect and has its personality, traits, and energy. Many people perform Navagraha worship, rituals, and poojas to enhance these celestial bodies' positive influences. This section discusses fundamental ways to connect with the Navagrahas and perform Navagraha worship and poojas.

Visiting Navagraha Temples

A common way to connect with the Navagrahas is by visiting their temples. Most Indian cities have Navagraha temples, with deities for different planets. For instance, the temple of Lord Shani (Saturn) is in Shani Shingnapur, Maharashtra, while the temple of Surya (Sun) is in Konark, Odisha. When visiting a Navagraha temple, devotees offer prayers, light oil lamps, and perform specific rituals according to the deity they worship.

Chanting Mantras

Mantras are powerful for connecting with the Navagrahas. Each planet has its mantra helping to balance its energy and enhance its positive influences. For instance, Lord Shani's mantra is "Om Shan Shanicharaya Namah." Lord Surya's mantra is "Om Hrim Hrim Suryaya Namah." Chanting these mantras daily or on specific days helps ward off the planet's negative influences and brings prosperity and success.

Performing Navagraha Pooja

Navagraha pooja is a ritual to worship the nine planets. It involves reciting mantras, offering flowers and fruits, lighting lamps and candles, and specific offerings to each planet according to its characteristics. Navagraha pooja is usually performed on special occasions like weddings, housewarming ceremonies, and during planetary transits that could be malefic.

Offering Flowers and Prasad

Offering flowers and prasadam (holy food) to the Navagrahas is essential to Navagraha worship. Each planet is associated with a specific flower and food item that pleases the deity and brings blessings. For instance, Lord Surya is worshipped with red flowers and dishes made with wheat. Lord Chandra (Moon) is offered white flowers and curd. Devotees offer these items during regular worship at home or during temple visits.

Observing Fasting and Abstinence

Navagraha worship observes fasts on specific days dedicated to each planet. For instance, Tuesdays are dedicated to Lord Mangal (Mars), while Saturdays are dedicated to Lord Shani (Saturn). Fasting on these days and abstaining from harmful activity helps appease the deity and mitigates the malefic effects of the planet on a person's life.

Worshipping the Sun on Sunday

The Sun is the most potent source of energy in the universe. Worshipping the Sun on Sundays is propitious and can give tremendous benefits. In addition to reciting the Sun mantra, devotees can perform Surya Namaskar (sun salutation) or sit in the sunlight to receive its benefits.

Navagraha worship is essential to Hindu spirituality. It balances the planets' energy and positively influences people's lives. With these practices, you can connect with the Navagrahas, seek their blessings, and live a fulfilling life. Whether visiting the temples, chanting mantras, performing poojas, or offering flowers and prasad, each activity significantly enhances the planets' positive effects. So, include Navagraha worship in your spiritual routine and experience its magic.

Navagraha Remedies

Are you looking for ways to overcome the negative influence of the nine planets on your life? Navagraha remedies, practiced since ancient times, can help balance your planet and bring success, health, and prosperity to your life. Navagrahas are nine heavenly bodies powerfully impacting people's lives; their strength or weakness can decide your fate. This section discusses the most effective Navagraha remedies to help you live a happy and fulfilling life.

Mantra Chanting and Meditation

Chanting the Navagraha mantras and meditating on their names can bring immense peace and calm to your life. Each planet has a specific mantra resonating with its vibrations, and reciting it can enhance its beneficial effects. For example, "Om Suryaya Namaha" is chanted for the Sun, and "Om Chandraaya Namaha" is for the Moon. Consult an astrologer or join a Navagraha mantra chanting group to know the correct pronunciation and ritual procedures.

Offering Prayers and Performing Pujas

Worshipping the Navagrahas, praying, and offerings help alleviate their adverse effects. Offer each planet flowers, fruits, incense, and other items, reciting their mantras. Performing pujas and homas dedicated to Navagrahas brings long-term benefits and prosperity.

Wearing Specific Gems and Rudraksha

Wearing specific gems and rudrakshas enhances the planets' positive effects. For example, wearing a ruby gemstone can strengthen the Sun, while a blue sapphire improves Saturn's influence. Wearing a 9-mukhi or 11-mukhi rudraksha provides positive vibrations and improves overall health and well-being.

Reciting Stotras of the Navagrahas

Stotras or hymns dedicated to the Navagrahas are also powerful for balancing their forces. Regularly reciting the Brihaspati Stotra, Shani Stotra, or Rahu Stotra can bring peace and prosperity to your life. Some astrologers suggest repeating the Navagraha Kavacha, a protective shield to repel negative influences.

Donations and Charity

Giving donations and performing charity work can mitigate the negative influence on the planet. You can donate to temples, feed people experiencing poverty, or contribute to a worthy cause. This act of kindness can earn positive karma and break the cycle of negative energies. The more generous you are, the better your planet will perform.

Whether through chanting mantras, offering prayers, wearing specific gems, or donating to charity, there are many ways to access the mystical powers of Navagrahas. Consult with a knowledgeable astrologer or a spiritual guide to select the best remedies for your specific planet positions and planetary periods. With faith and regular practice, Navagraha remedies can help you unlock the path to success, happiness, and abundance.

When and How to Start Navagraha Worship

Navagraha worship balances the influence of these celestial bodies, leading to a happier and more prosperous life. The Navagrahas, including the Sun, Moon, Mars, Mercury, Jupiter, Venus, Saturn, Rahu, and Ketu, significantly impact people's lives. This section discusses when and how to start Navagraha worship and how it can help you identify and deal with problems in your life.

- **Determine Your Rashi and Grahas:** The first step toward Navagraha worship is determining your Rashi (or zodiac sign) and the grahas influencing your life. Several websites and apps can help you determine your Rashi and grahas based on your date of birth. You can understand how the Navagrahas affect your life with this information.

- **Identifying the Problem Areas in Your Life:** The next step is to identify the problem areas the Navagrahas influence. For example, if Saturn is causing delays or obstacles in your career, you should address this issue through Navagraha worship. By identifying the grahas causing the problems, you can focus on worshipping those Navagrahas.

- **Consulting an Astrologer or Guru for Assistance:** If you are new to Navagraha worship, consult an astrologer or guru for guidance. They will help you identify the grahas affecting your life and recommend appropriate remedies to balance their influence. They might suggest specific mantras, yantras, or rituals to help you achieve your desired results.

- **Choosing the Appropriate Remedies and Solutions:** Based on the guidance of your astrologer or guru, you can select the appropriate remedies and solutions to counteract the Navagrahas' negative influence. These remedies include wearing gemstones, performing mantras, or observing specific rituals. You might need to make lifestyle changes or restructure your routines to align with the Navagrahas' positive influence.
- **Performing the Rituals as Instructed:** Once you have identified the appropriate remedies, performing the rituals as instructed is vital. This involves following specific guidelines and observing certain fasting periods or purification practices. Navagraha worship is a disciplined practice requiring dedication and commitment. Adhering to your astrologer or guru's instructions is essential for optimal results.
- **Keeping a Record of Your Experiences and Progress:** As you practice Navagraha worship, keeping a record of your experiences and progress is advisable. It will help you identify areas for improvement and track your journey toward a happier and more prosperous life. You should periodically visit your astrologer or guru to adjust your remedies based on your progress.

By identifying your Rashi and grahas and consulting an astrologer or guru, you can choose appropriate remedies and solutions to address the problem areas in your life. As you perform the rituals and observe the guidelines, keeping a record of your progress and experiences is essential. Navagraha worship requires discipline and dedication, but it can lead to a happier, more prosperous life aligned with the positive influence of the Navagrahas.

Tips for Navagraha Worship

Acknowledging and appeasing the nine planetary gods, you reduce astrological afflictions, overcome obstacles, and can enjoy enhanced success, happiness, and well-being. However, conducting the ritual with the utmost care, dedication, and positivity is essential to reap the benefits of the Navagraha. This section explores tips to strengthen your connection with the Navagrahas and enhance your worship's efficacy.

Have a Positive Mindset: The first and foremost tip for successful Navagraha worship is cultivating a positive mindset. Before you begin the ritual, take a few deep breaths, and think of the positive changes you wish to bring into your life. Focus on the benefits of worshipping the Navagrahas and believe in their powers to help you overcome obstacles.

Be Determined and Dedicated: Navagraha worship is not a one-time affair. It requires time, effort, and dedication. Set a specific time and place for your daily worship and stick to it, regardless of your schedule or mood. Push yourself to complete the ritual with sincerity and devotion, and do not let laziness or other distractions get in the way.

Follow the Instructions Carefully: All Navagraha worship rituals follow strict guidelines prescribed in the Vedic scriptures. Read and understand these guidelines carefully to ensure the efficacy of your worship. Follow the mantra recitation, yantra placement, and other instructions precisely, and avoid improvisations or shortcuts unless an expert recommends them.

Avoid Distractions and Disruptions: During your Navagraha worship, switch off your phone, TV, or other devices that could disturb your concentration. Choose a quiet, clean, and well-ventilated space for your worship, away from clutter or disturbances. Avoid negative thoughts, emotions, or conversations during prayer.

- **Be Consistent with Your Worship:** Navagraha worship yields the best results when done consistently for an extended period. Make it a habit to perform the ritual daily or on special planetary occasions. If you cannot complete the worship, seek advice from an astrologer or priest.

- **Stay Calm and Meditate:** One of the primary objectives of Navagraha worship is to attain inner peace and harmony. Practice deep breathing, mindfulness, or meditation before or after your worship. Focus on your breath, chant mantras, or visualize the positive effects of your worship on your life. This will help you stay calm, centered, and aligned with the planets' energies.

- **Seek Help When Required:** Navagraha worship is a complex practice requiring extensive knowledge, skill, and experience. If you are new to this practice or face obstacles in your worship, do not hesitate to seek guidance from a reliable astrologer or priest. They will help you with personalized rituals, yantra

energization, and other methods to enhance your worship's efficacy.
- **Enjoy the Process of Worship:** Remember, Navagraha worship is not a means to an end but an enriching experience. Enjoy connecting with the planetary gods, learning about their attributes and attributes, and seeking their blessings for your well-being. Have faith in the divine powers of the Navagrahas and trust that they will show you the right path in life.

Navagraha worship is a powerful practice to help you overcome the adverse effects of planetary alignments and achieve success, happiness, and well-being. However, to harness the full potential of this practice, you must approach it with dedication, positivity, and consistency. Follow these tips, and do not hesitate to seek guidance when required. With the right mindset and efforts, you can strengthen your connection with the Navagrahas and unlock their divine blessings.

Results of Navagraha Worship

According to Hindu mythology, each planet represents different aspects of life, and worshipping them can help you succeed and overcome obstacles. Navagraha worship has been followed for ages, and the results have been staggering. This section delves deeper into the positive effects of Navagraha worship and how it can benefit you.

- **Positive Effects on Health:** The most significant benefit of Navagraha worship is its positive impact on people's health. Each planet represents different body parts, and their worship helps maintain good health. For example, worshipping Mars can mitigate disorders related to the blood, while Venus is associated with the reproductive system. Similarly, worshipping Jupiter can cure liver-related ailments. Navagraha worship regulates bodily functions and maintains good health.
- **Clears Obstacles in Life:** Everyone encounters obstacles in life, but Navagraha worship can eliminate them. By worshipping the planets, you can minimize the adverse effects of their malefic influence and enhance the positive impact of their benefic influence. For example, Saturn is associated with obstacles and delays, so worshipping it can alleviate those problems. Navagraha worship helps eliminate barriers and bring success and prosperity.

- **Financial Stability:** Financial stability is something everyone craves. Worshipping planets like Jupiter and Venus can help bring wealth and prosperity. Jupiter is associated with wealth and affluence, and worshipping it can bring good luck in wealth. Venus is associated with luxury and comfort. Honoring these planets invites financial stability and material prosperity into your life.
- **Success in Career and Education:** Everyone aspires to success in their career and education. Navagraha worship can achieve this goal. Planets like the Sun and Mars are associated with leadership and courage. Enhance their personality traits aligned with those planets by worshipping them. Similarly, Mercury is associated with intelligence and wisdom; worshipping it improves your educational prospects. Worshipping these planets can help you achieve great success in your career and education.
- **Better Relationships with Family and Friends:** Navagraha worship helps improve relationships with family and friends. Planets like the Moon and Venus are associated with emotions and harmony. Worshipping them enhances compassion and love toward your loved ones. Similarly, Jupiter is associated with devotion and trust, and worshipping it can help improve interpersonal relationships. Navagraha worship brings harmony and peace to your life.
- **Increased Spiritual Awareness:** Navagraha worship helps enhance spiritual awareness. Planets like the Sun and Moon are associated with divine energies and cosmic consciousness. You can gain insight into your spiritual journey and strengthen the divine connection by worshipping them. It helps you stay grounded and open to the universe's higher forces. The Navagraha worship increases spiritual awareness and connectedness with the divine.
- **Improvement in Doshas:** Navagraha worship can balance the doshas in your life. The nine planets represent different aspects of life, and their worship can bring harmony to your life. Balance the three doshas by honoring these planets, including Vata, Pitta, and Kapha. The nine planets have different attributes regulating the doshas in your body, bringing peace

and harmony. Navagraha worship alleviates imbalances in the doshas and balances a person's life.

Navagraha worship is a traditional practice proven immensely beneficial for those who follow it. Worshipping the nine celestial bodies can enhance various aspects of life, including health, wealth, career, and relationships. You can minimize the negative influence of the malefic planets and reap the benefits of the benefic planets by worshipping the planets.

This chapter covered the essential aspects of Navagraha worship, including how to do it, remedies to help mitigate the adverse effects of a planet, and the results of Navagraha worship. This chapter provided helpful information about this ancient practice and encouraged you to explore its potential further. You can unlock the nine planets' divine powers and bring happiness, success, and prosperity to your life. Namaste.

Conclusion

Vedic astrology is an ancient science that has helped people understand the mysteries of the universe for thousands of years. Rahu and Ketu are the most important to consider in understanding the planets. These shadow planets represent a powerful force in life, and understanding their influence can help make sense of the challenges and opportunities that come your way. This guide explored Rahu and Ketu's significance, including their role in natal charts, the Nakshatras they rule over, related karmic patterns, and much more.

There's plenty of complexity when understanding Rahu and Ketu in astrology. These two planetary energies are often seen as opposites - Rahu represents ambition, desire, and material success, while Ketu embodies spiritual pursuits, detachment, and attachments. You can discover ultimate harmony in your life by recognizing the importance of worldly success.

The dance between Rahu and Ketu is fascinating, full of intricate movements and unexpected twists and turns. But beyond its aesthetic beauty, this dance holds great significance for those seeking to uncover their true destiny. By studying the rhythms and patterns of this cosmic duo, you gain a deeper understanding of the forces that drive you and the paths you are meant to follow. Whether struggling to find direction in life or searching for a more profound purpose, Rahu and Ketu's guidance can lead closer to greater self-awareness and fulfillment.

This guide began with an overview of Vedic astrology, the ancient Indian practice that relies heavily on Rahu and Ketu. Then it took an in-depth look at these two shadow planets, including their qualities and roles in birth charts. It explored the associated Nakshatras and the karmic patterns in their placements. This guide provided remedies for malefic Rahu and Ketu and suggestions for Navagraha worship and other remedies.

Working with Rahu and Ketu for personal growth helps balance worldly pursuits with spiritual fulfillment and better understand yourselves and your place in the universe. The insights gained from these two planets help you make wise decisions and discover your life path. This guide provided a glossary of terms helping you further understand Vedic astrology.

By learning and applying the knowledge in this guide, you are well on your way to understanding Rahu and Ketu's significance in Vedic astrology. With their guidance, you can embrace the joys and challenges of life, discover your true purpose, and progress toward achieving higher self-awareness. Life can be a complex journey, but with these two shadow planets, you can navigate it all with greater clarity and confidence. So, embrace your destiny and get ready to dive into the mystical world of Rahu and Ketu.

Glossary of Terms

Vedic astrology is a vast field of knowledge; it is easy to get lost in the jargon and terminology in this practice. Understanding these terms and their meanings gives you a better perspective on your horoscope and how to use it to improve your life. This section includes terms, words, and phrases commonly used in Vedic astrology, their meanings, and pronunciations.

- **Agni:** Fire also refers to the Sun. Pronunciation: AG-nee
- **Bhava:** One of the most critical concepts in Vedic astrology. It relates to the "house" or area of life a planet occupies in a chart.
- **Dasha:** This system predicts future events based on the planets' positions and their effects on particular houses.
- **Dharma:** One of the four main goals in life according to Vedic astrology. It represents a person's dharma or purpose. Pronunciation: DHAR-mah
- **Doshas:** These are planetary imbalances causing difficulties in life.
- **Ganesha:** The Hindu god of wisdom, often called upon to help solve complex astrological problems.
- **Gochara:** The astrological term for transits or the planets' movement through the zodiac.
- **Graha:** The word means *planet* and refers to the major planets in the solar system. Pronunciation: GRAH-hah

- **Graha Chakra:** The planetary chart in Vedic astrology to predict the future. Pronunciation: GRAH-hah CHAH-krah
- **Jyotish:** Vedic astrology, the science of light. Pronunciation: JYO-tish
- **Karma:** The effects of past actions in this life or a previous one. Pronunciation: KAHR-mah
- **Ketu:** One of the nine major planets in Vedic astrology, representing spirituality, moksha (liberation), and other mystical experiences.
- **Kundali:** The Vedic astrology term for a birth chart indicating the position of all planets at birth. Pronunciation: KUUN-dah-lee
- **Lagna:** This term refers to the ascendant or rising sign in a chart, which determines a person's personality traits.
- **Muhurta:** Selecting an auspicious time for important events like marriage, travel, and other ceremonies. Pronunciation: moo-HUR-tah
- **Nadi:** An ancient astrology system using palmistry to predict the future. Pronunciation: NAH-dee
- **Nakshatra:** These are the 27 constellations or star signs in Vedic astrology. Pronunciation: NAHK-shah-trah
- **Rashi:** A Zodiac sign based on the planets' and stars' positions. Pronunciation: RAH-shee
- **Ritus:** The Vedic astrology term for the six seasons of the year, divided by two equinoxes and two solstices.
- **Tithi:** A lunar day to determine the exact time of a planetary transit.
- **Vedas:** The sacred Hindu scriptures, the earliest, were written around 1500 BC. Pronunciation: VAY-dahs
- **Yoga:** A combination of two or more planets in a chart that can cause powerful effects.

Here's another book by Mari Silva that you might like

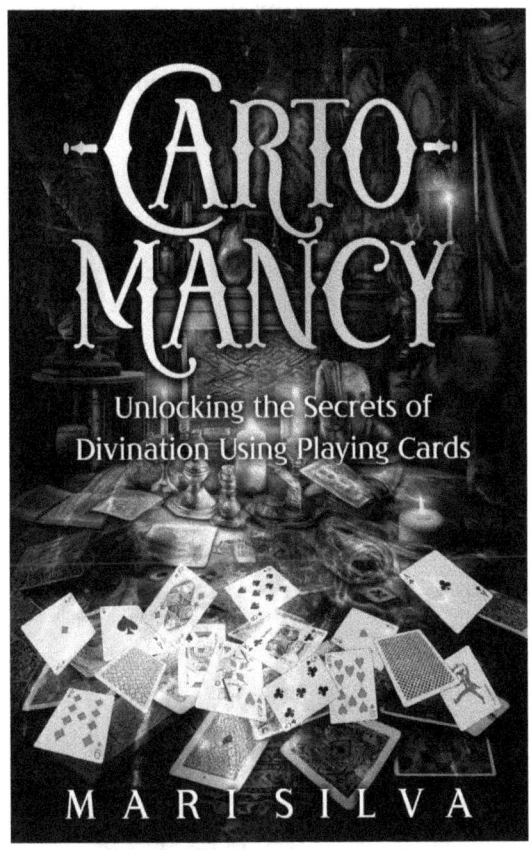

Your Free Gift
(only available for a limited time)

Thanks for getting this book! If you want to learn more about various spirituality topics, then join Mari Silva's community and get a free guided meditation MP3 for awakening your third eye. This guided meditation mp3 is designed to open and strengthen ones third eye so you can experience a higher state of consciousness. Simply visit the link below the image to get started.

https://spiritualityspot.com/meditation

Or, Scan the QR code!

References

(N.d.-b). Outlookindia.com. https://www.outlookindia.com/outlook-spotlight/a-brief-about-rahu-it-s-influences-over-our-life-news-200762

Astrology, T. O. I. (2020, December 1). What is Rahu? How to reduce malefic effects of Rahu? Times Of India. https://timesofindia.indiatimes.com/astrology/planets-transits/what-is-rahu-how-to-reduce-malefic-effects-of-rahu/articleshow/79510254.cms

Eclipsing effects of rahu and Ketu in astrology. (2021, October 6). GaneshaSpeaks. https://www.ganeshaspeaks.com/astrology/planets/nodes/

Gupta, K. (2021, July 12). Rahu and Ketu gives positive results in these houses - AstroTalk. AstroTalk Blog - Online Astrology Consultation with Astrologer; AstroTalk. https://astrotalk.com/astrology-blog/good-house-placement-for-rahu-and-ketu-in-kundli/

Monk, I. [@IndianMonk]. (2022, March 19). Rahu and Ketu : The two lunar nodes. Youtube. https://www.youtube.com/watch?v=sid3Z4xm6uE

Rahu and ketu. (2014, May 16). Vedic Astrology | Astrology Readings and Learn Astrology; Family Constellations. https://vedicastrology.net.au/blog/vedic-articles/rahu-and-ketu/

Rahu-Ketu: (2022, September 6). Amarujala. https://www.amarujala.com/photo-gallery/astrology/predictions-about-rahu-and-ketu-in-kundali-know-all-about-effect-of-rahu-ketu-in-life

Yoga member-Noelle. (2017, October 29). The myth of RAHU and KETU: The Lunar Nodes. The Yoga Sanctuary. https://www.theyogasanctuary.biz/the-myth-of-rahu-and-ketu-the-lunar-nodes